Tina Modotti

Tina Modotti

A LIFE

by Pino Cacucci

Translated from the Italian
by Patricia J. Duncan

St. Martin's Press ⚓ New York

Design by Ellen R. Sasahara

Grateful acknowledgment is given for permission to reprint from the following works:

Canto LXXXVI by Ezra Pound from *The Cantos of Ezra Pound.* Copyright © 1934, 1948 by Ezra Pound. Reprinted by permission of New Directions Publishing Corp. "Tina Modotti Is Dead" by Pablo Neruda from *Residence on Earth.* Copyright © 1973 by Pablo Neruda and Donald D. Walsh. Reprinted by permission of New Directions Publishing Corp.

Letters by Tina Modotti and Edward Weston throughout, and the letter from Roubaix de l'Abrie Richey to Weston, are reprinted courtesy of the Edward Weston Archive, Center for Creative Photography, with the following exceptions: the letter by Tina Modotti on page 28 is from *Edward Weston: 70 Photographs* by Ben Maddow (Boston: Aperture/NY Graphic Society, 1978); the letters by Edward Weston on pages 35, 37, 44 © 1981 by Edward Weston. Arizona Board of Regents, Center for Creative Photography. Reprinted by permission.

Library of Congress Cataloging-in-Publication Data

Cacucci, Pino.
   [Tina Modotti. English]
   Tina Modotti : a life / Pino Cacucci ; translated by Patricia J. Duncan. —1st U.S. ed.
     p. cm.
   ISBN 0-312-20036-6
   1. Modotti, Tina, 1896–1942. 2. Women photographers—Italy—Biography. 3. Women photographers—Mexico—Biography. 4. Photographers—Mexico—Biography. 5. Women communists—Italy—Biography. 6. Women communists—Mexico—Biography. 7. Communists—Mexico—Biography. I. Title.
TR140.M58C32 13   1999
770'.92—dc21
[b]   98-31175
                                         CIP

First published in the United States by St. Martin's Press
First published in Italy under the title *Tina* by Pino Cacucci, Interno Giallo Editore, s.r.l., Milano, 1991

First U.S. Edition: March 1999

10 9 8 7 6 5 4 3 2 1

Contents

Prologue   1

Part One: The Young Revolutionary   15

Part Two: Into the Maze   47

Part Three: Photography and Militancy   79

Part Four: Crossing Borders   113

Part Five: A Kind of Homecoming   175

Epilogue   206

Selected Bibliography   209

Index   213

About the Author and Translator   225

Tina Modotti

Prologue

It was the night of January 10, 1929, shortly before ten o'clock. The heart of the Mexican capital was deserted. A few cars moved silently along the vast Paseo de la Reforma. Only a few passersby, shivering from the cold, and one last drunk who was cursing at a closed *cantina*, were out.

A pack of stray dogs crossed Abraham Gonzáles Street, hesitating under the light that filtered out of a bakery. They dug through a pile of garbage at the intersection of Morelos Avenue. The leader of the group stiffened. He smelled the dry, frigid air. He looked down the street and saw three figures approaching in the darkness. He must have given an all but imperceptible signal, and the other five followed him to a clearing filled with rubbish, under the protection of the harsh light of a street lamp. Two boys appeared in a doorway, picked up some stones, and threw them, laughing, but the dogs were already far away. The boys sat back down in the doorway, waiting for the night to give them a reason to flee their miserable, run-down room at the back of the patio.

Two men and a woman appeared out of the darkness. One of the men was young, tall, athletic-looking, with a firm step. The other was short, his face hidden by a wide-brimmed felt hat. They were arguing and cursing. The woman was small, slender; her face was pale and her look sad. The two boys observed her, exchanging a look of complicity. "*Tá guapísima*," the older one whispered, as if he were an expert. Yes, the other boy thought, she is beautiful. She must be foreign. And the two men too. Or maybe not; maybe the one with the hat is Mexican. The light from the street lamp revealed for a moment his black mustache and dark eyes.

The baker wiped away the sweat and moved a few steps toward the door. He took a deep breath of the clear, cool air. When he was about to turn around something caught his attention—stifled shouting—and the three figures stopped in the middle of the street.

He heard a few angry words that were impossible to make out. The man in the black hat had one hand at his waist. The other man began to react instinctively, but he seemed paralyzed by disbelief. A shot rang out, its flash magnified by the darkness. The tall young man shrank, swayed, but his muscular body supported him; he struggled to hurl himself toward the walls of the houses, in search of a nonexistent refuge. A second shot. He fell to his knees, got up again, and staggered a few meters. Then he seemed to weaken, groping for support in the air.

The woman remained motionless beneath the light of the street lamp, petrified, with an expression of terrified astonishment. A few eternal seconds elapsed. Only then, when she saw the young man hunched up on the pavement, his hands pressed against his chest, could she feel her blood flow again, and she took her first, uncertain step, trembling. She looked around, nervous and frantic. The man in the hat had disappeared. She ran forward and dropped to her knees, grasped her comrade's head, stroked it lightly, and squeezed his bloody hand, which continued searching for support so he could get up again.

"Tina . . . I'm dying, Tina."

The woman kissed him on the lips and the forehead and ran her hand through his thick, curly hair. She saw her own tears fall on the man's cheeks, and she said, in a muffled voice: "No, Julio . . . you're too young . . . you can't die like this."

He tried desperately to keep talking, but his lungs were as tight as knots, and his throat was paralyzed from the cold, a cold that had overtaken his now unfeeling legs and was rising to his heart. He opened his eyes, pulled her to him violently. She leaned over and caressed him softly, nodding and comforting him.

The man behind the desk studied the pamphlet carefully. He had already read it several times, but he kept glancing at the threatening sentences, shaking his head.

"They didn't waste any time," he said quietly.

The other man stopped leafing through the files and removed his glasses. "They have already begun to mobilize," he said, "and if we arrest that—you can imagine the consequences."

The first man nodded and sighed. Then he addressed a soldier. "It's okay. Bring her in."

Two uniformed agents brought the woman in and showed her to a chair. She had dark rings under her eyes, a swarthy complexion, and wrinkles like scars at the corners of her mouth and around her eyelids. It would have been difficult to identify her as the young woman of the previous night. In just a few hours she seemed to have aged many years.

"I am Judge Alfredo Pino Camara, of the Second Penal Division," the man said, getting up. He walked around the desk and pointed to another man.

"My assistant, Mr. Alfonso Casamadrid."

The man bowed respectfully, barely getting up from his chair.

"Your name, please?"

"Tina Modotti," the woman murmured without taking her eyes off the sky that filled the large window.

The judge went over to her. When she finally looked at him, he picked up a piece of paper from the desk and asked her indifferently, "Why did you say yesterday that your name was Rose Smith Santarini?"

The woman held his stare but did not respond.

"All right," the judge said, moving behind her. "I understand. You are involved in political activities, activities that until now my government has also participated in, or at least tolerated. Revolutionary Mexico extends its hospitality to everyone, without discrimination, and it supports the struggle of the American nations against colonialism."

He paused, then moved in front of her again and looked straight at her.

"And if what your comrades say is true, we would be prepared to strongly condemn the Cuban government of General Machado, but . . ."

The judge folded his arms and looked her up and down.

"But . . . unfortunately we have some doubts about the political version of this murder."

The woman made a slight gesture of defiance. She was about to say something, but she held back. The judge picked up a large envelope and with deliberate slowness untied the ribbon that held it closed. He removed the Colt .45, model 1911, and held it out in the palm of his hand.

"Do you recognize this gun?"

She nodded affirmatively. She took a deep breath, raised her head, and looked at the heavy automatic.

"It was taken from my apartment this morning," she said, "when I was arrested."

"Señora Modotti, you have not been arrested," the judge hastily corrected her, and then added, "as long as you agree to cooperate."

"What do you want to know?"

"Just a detailed account of the incident. That's all."

She turned to look out the window again. Staring into space for a few seconds, she closed her eyes, sighed, and began to talk in a weak voice, exhausted.

"We were returning home. We were almost there. We . . . I live at number thirty-one. . . . He came up from behind. I didn't get a good look at him. I just heard the shots, and . . . and then Julio fell, and I threw myself on him."

"Do you mean to say they opened fire from a moving car?" the assistant interjected.

Tina nodded. After a long pause she added, "But I wouldn't be able to tell you what kind of car it was . . . at the time everything was very confusing. . . . It was dark, and—"

"In short, if I understand correctly," the judge interrupted her, "you were walking next to the victim, Señor Mella, and there was no one else with you. . . . Is that right?"

She stared at him, emerging from the painful fog that enveloped her. She frowned and said, "Of course there was no one else. I don't understand."

The judge stared at her for a while. Then he looked over at his assistant and seemed to signal for him to pay attention. He asked, "At the time of the crime, were you walking next to the victim, or were you a few steps away from him?"

"I was holding on to his arm," she responded wearily, the words dragging.

"Ah, so, then, very close. And on what side?"

The woman seemed to focus on the image of the man questioning her, as if each question were pulling her out of the remote place in which she had taken refuge. She looked at one hand, then the other, and said, "The left, I think . . . yes, I was on the left."

"On his left," the judge repeated, nodding. "And where were you coming from?"

"From Reforma, and at the intersection of Morelos there—"

She stopped, noticing the judge's disgusted expression, one of affected disappointment, certainly false. The assistant, who seemed to have received the invisible order he was waiting for, shook his head regretfully. He picked up a piece of paper and handed it to the woman.

"Would you be kind enough, Señora Modotti, to have a look at *this*?"

It was a statement from Anacleto Rodríguez and José Flores, both minors, residing at 22 Abraham Gonzáles Street, who stated that they had seen three people, two men and one woman, coming from the direction of Bucareli Street, arguing excitedly. Then one of the two men had shot the other and disappeared on foot.

"So Señora Modotti, were you coming from Reforma or Bucareli?" the judge asked, suddenly abandoning his disgusted expression.

"I don't know. I thought it was Reforma, but what difference—"

"It makes a *big* difference," the judge pressed. "Because, you see, I find it very difficult to understand how you could be on the victim's left and not see the person who fired the gun, considering that one of the shots went through Mella's left arm. That is, the one you were holding on to, as you just stated. If they had opened fire at that time, you should have seen them. Or else the murderer shot when the victim was already trying to run away, which would completely remove the element of surprise."

The judge and the witness looked at each other carefully. Neither one looked down.

"So, then, Señora Modotti, if you were coming from Bucareli, and you were on the east side of Abraham Gonzáles Street, the car should have passed on your right. And the victim was shot from the left. Do you want to tell me now who murdered Julio Antonio Mella, and why?"

The woman looked down, but her face showed no signs of giving in. Softly, almost whispering, she stated, "I don't know who murdered Julio. Those two boys testified falsely. I have nothing else to say."

Judge Camara issued an order putting Tina on probation, which was tantamount to house arrest, under the constant surveillance of two agents.

Mella's autopsy established that the first shot had passed through his left arm near his elbow, penetrating the intestine, and the second shot had perforated one of his lungs. He had been shot from behind, and he died a few hours later, when they were trying to extract the bullets in the emergency room at Hospital Juárez. Ballistic experts harbored no doubts: The bullets were .38 caliber and had certainly been fired from a revolver and not an automatic, although no cartridges were found. Finding the Colt .45 in Modotti's apartment now lost importance. But a new witness came forward to reinforce the interrogators' suspicions: Luis Herberiche, a German immigrant who managed a bakery on Abraham Gonzáles Street, confirmed the boys' statements and added even more precise details about the man he had seen arguing excitedly with Mella. In a confrontation with Modotti, he stated, "I have no reason to lie or deceive justice. I am a businessman who does not like to be mixed up in these matters. If it were up to me, I would never have come to testify. But what I said is the truth, and I stand by it. I am sorry for contradicting the señora. I am mixed up in this situation, and I will surely have to leave my job."

In the meantime the newspapers were digging into Tina's private life, focusing only on those aspects that could cause a scandal. The *Excelsior,* one of the most widely circulated papers in Mexico, obtained photos in which Tina appeared completely nude. For the mores of the time, this equaled an irreversible condemnation.

> We have looked at two photographs that are truly revealing: the first is of Julio Antonio Mella, the second is of Tina Modotti, his lover. Both show these individuals completely nude, in unbecoming positions that would be plausible if dealing with a shameless and infamous person, not an "apostle of Communism, guide, inspirer and muse of revolutionary splendor." And this fact alone would be enough, among decent people, to deprive Mella of posthumous honors and to relegate his concubine to the category of women who sell love and rent out their own bodies.

The press unhesitatingly supported the theory of a crime of passion. As evidence of her immoral and "promiscuous" conduct, they published some letters from Modotti to Xavier Guerrero, a Mexican Communist leader, with whom she had had a previous relationship before he left for Moscow. The letters praised his charm and his cold and contemptuous manner with interrogators. The newspapers demanded that she be forced to reveal everything she knew. Concurrently, the press used the shooting to launch a campaign against the political refugees and the "agents of Communism" who created disorder in the capital.

The response was a feverish mobilization of the Mexican Left, which openly accused Cuban dictator Gerardo Machado of being the one who had ordered Mella's assassination, and refuted all the accusations against Modotti, one after another, maintaining that it was an unprecedented setup designed to blame the crime on the revolutionary movement and to expel refugees, who had a sound base of popular and institutional support in Mexico. The Mexican government found itself in a serious predicament: On the one hand, Cuban Ambassador Mascaró lodged a formal protest at what he characterized as "unfounded scandalous accusations against the government of a friendly country," and on the other, it recognized that the inalienable principle of hospitality for political refugees from any creed or country was at stake—a fundamental right ratified by the laws of revolutionary Mexico.

Rendering the situation even more delicate was the entrance on the scene of Diego Rivera, an artist who was revered in intellectual circles and who had great popular charisma. Rivera accused the police of losing precious time with its nonsense about a crime of passion, giving the perpetrators time to erase possible evidence. He defended Tina's honor and reputation, attacking the moral baseness of the yellow, tabloid press; and, in regard to the "indecent" photos, he went personally to the office of the *Excelsior* and asked to see the editor, Rodrigo de Llano. The *Excelsior* did not dare become an enemy of such a famous and beloved figure as Rivera, and the next day it published his statement almost in its entirety:

> Some nude photographs found in the home of Señora Modotti have been used by one of your writers as a basis for describing the above-mentioned señora and Julio Antonio Mella with epithets that for me are an insult to the memory of a dead man and a woman who is presently not able to defend herself.
>
> What's more, this unheard-of attack represents a very serious precedent for the free professional practice of all those working in the artistic field, from sculpture and painting to dance and theater. It is absurd to qualify the nude as immoral, as in that case at least fifty percent of the most beautiful artistic works in the world should be condemned.
>
> The photographs that show Tina Modotti nude are the work of the master Edward Weston, recognized as one of the best artists in his field. Señora Modotti posed for him as a professional model. As for the photo of Julio Antonio Mella, it was taken several years ago, when he entered the athletic club for rowers in Havana. Mella was one of the best rowers in that city, and in the photograph he appears nude at the door of a shower, something the rules required in order to be able to enter.
>
> Tina Modotti also posed for me, and if you need another picture of her without clothes, go photograph my mural at the Universidad de Chapingo!

In fact, the figure of Modotti embodied *La Tierra*, the mural that still remains in Chapingo. She had also posed for Diego Rivera in other works, like that in the Palacio Nacional, where she is depicted distributing guns to rebels. But the image of Modotti, defended so fervently by the muralist, was later tarnished by the appearance of an extremely mysterious man who had undertaken activities that were anything but clear.

In one of Mella's pockets the police found a card with a name and the address of a meeting place. The card referred to the Cuban José Magriñat, a presumed fugitive from the dictatorship and considered by Communists to be a spy for Machado and an agent provocateur. According to Modotti, Magriñat had looked for Mella to warn him of the imminent attack on him. The meeting had taken place the very afternoon of January 10, in the bar La India, on the corner of Bolívar and República de Salvador Streets. There Magriñat had told Mella that Cuba had sent two hired assassins to kill him, without specifying how he had found this out. Judge Camara ordered a confrontation between Modotti and Magriñat.

"Let the record reflect: Both witnesses agree that they have not met before today."

The judge looked up, gazing at Magriñat and then at Modotti. She nodded, raising a cigarette to her lips. She could not hide the tremor in her hands, and she appeared increasingly nervous before the arrogant Cuban.

"Señor Magriñat, the witness present here maintains that you had a meeting with the victim at the bar La India in order to warn him about a plot against him. Can you confirm this?"

Magriñat threw his head back, laughing provocatively.

"Do you find this funny, Señor Magriñat?"

The Cuban quickly became serious. He stared at the judge and folded his arms across his chest.

"Absolutely not, Your Honor. At best I find it ludicrous. I met Mella at La India, but only because he had asked to see me. Señora Modotti has simply reversed the facts of the matter . . . and I wonder what interest she might have in doing so."

He turned around toward Modotti, who avoided his gaze.

"The reason for the meeting?" the judge asked.

"He asked me to send a cable to the Cuban newspaper *La Semana*, denying that he had offended the flag of our country. This had to do with something that took place some time ago, an unpleasant incident during a party at the Cuban Embassy here. The Cuban government staged a nationalistic incident, accusing Mella of having insulted and vilified the flag. . . . I agreed to help him, and I assured him that I would do everything I could to see that his version of events was published."

The judge nodded and looked at Modotti, who had lit another cigarette. For the first time, the woman was displaying an uneasiness that contrasted with her usual closed and distant behavior.

"So, Señor Magriñat, you deny having referred to two hired assassins sent by President Machado?"

Magriñat shifted impatiently, slapped his legs and interrupted the judge. "Who made up such nonsense?! This is the first I've heard of it."

"Julio told me right after the meeting," Modotti interjected, addressing the judge. "And he added that he didn't want to give too much importance to what José Magriñat said because he didn't consider him trustworthy."

Magriñat slowly turned around to face Modotti.

"Not trustworthy? And from whose point of view, Señora Modotti? For what purpose?"

Then he addressed the judge: "I had nothing to do with the political activities of poor Mella and his lover. . . . If I am here, it is only because I agreed to help him, at his request. Mella called me a few days earlier, begging to see me because he wanted to ask me a favor. Unfortunately I wasn't able to make the meeting, so the next day I called the number he had given me. A woman answered the phone, and she gave me a new meeting time."

The judge looked over at Modotti, who continued shifting in her chair and wringing her hands.

"Are you the one who answered the phone?"

"I don't know what you're talking about," she responded, gesturing toward Magriñat without looking at him. "I never received a phone call like that and I never arranged a meeting for Julio."

"Do you still have that number, Señor Magriñat?"

"I'm sorry," the Cuban responded, "I don't remember it, and I lost the paper on which I wrote it down."

The judge got up. "Well, Señores, that's all for today," he said to the two agents responsible for keeping an eye on Modotti and escorting her to her apartment. Magriñat did not take his eyes off her, showing off his self-confidence.

"Señor Magriñat," the judge said, stopping him at the door, "I have to ask that you remain available to us. Do not leave the city, and inform us of your whereabouts at all times. We may need to locate you at any time."

Magriñat shrugged and smiled.

"*I* have nothing to hide. But unfortunately for her, I have already reported everything I know about this matter."

The Cuban left, putting on his hat. In the corridor journalists rushed toward him to interview him. He made his way through, asking them politely to let him pass, while the photographers' flashes went off all around. They all wanted a statement, asked him questions, and begged him at least to comment.

Magriñat stopped in the doorway and said loudly: "Everyone knows that Mella's woman was involved with another man. Go look for him if you want to know anything else."

He left abruptly, without giving anyone time to ask for an explanation.

The following day, the headlines again vigorously proclaimed the theory that it had been a crime of passion.

Support for Modotti immediately became more general, turning into a campaign against the Cuban dictatorship and the Mexican police, accused of paying witnesses to hide the real nature of the homicide. The funeral service for Julio Antonio Mella became the pretext for a large demonstration during which incidents and riots erupted. A corps of firemen was used to charge the demonstrators; structured like a government militia, they burst into the demonstration aboard trucks, using hoses and ax handles.

Witnesses came forward to testify in favor of Modotti. The Right maintained that they were leftist militants whom the Communist Party had convinced to make statements in support of their theory. On the other hand, the interrogators could not ignore the testimony of Rogelio Teurbe Tolón, the young Cuban refugee who stated that Mella had also spoken to him about the rumor of some hired assassins sent to kill him. And he added that he thought Magriñat was working for General Machado's government, accusing him of having organized the attack.

The testimony of Virginia Castaños, a woman who lived at 19 Abraham Gonzáles Street, was decisive. She stated that on the night of January 10, when she was about to go to bed, she heard two explosions. When she went to the balcony to look out, she saw a young man running toward Morelos Avenue. He then fell to the ground at once and was helped by a woman. Virginia Castaños stated that she had heard him shout. "Let everyone know: He ordered me to assassinate the entire government of Cuba."

The political trial resumed importance. The trial judge revoked the restrictions on Modotti's freedom and decided to delve into some of the unsavory aspects of Magriñat's character. Customers of some of the bars the Cuban used to frequent maintained that they had often heard him talk with a couple of "suspicious" individuals about "people who must be eliminated." There was no doubt that Magriñat was tied to shady activities, a kind of parasite who took advantage of the frenzied climate among the Cuban refugees; but it was quite rare for a "secret agent" of the dictator to be involved in barroom boasting. At any rate, in subsequent interrogations, the Cuban contradicted himself, and the judge ordered his arrest as a precaution to prevent possible evidence from being contaminated.

The press suddenly changed its target. Leaving Modotti now, they portrayed Magriñat as the new monster on the front page. Repugnant details were disclosed about him, such as the fact that he demanded "services from the wives of men for whom he did favors"; the most vulgar aspects of his behavior were dug up, and once again the focus turned to the immoral conduct of the accused rather than the evidence against him.

The trial ran aground in a few weeks. Magriñat was freed, witnesses on both sides continued to maintain their positions, and nothing new emerged. The crisis in relations with the Cuban government and the growing protest against the Mexican police demanded that at least one head fall: The man in charge of the Security Commission, Valente Quintana, was dismissed from his post.

La Prensa was the last newspaper to be interested in the matter, interviewing Modotti in order to point out that it had been the only media organization that had respected her person even "within the parameters of the situation":

> After days of suffering over the loss of the man who, in her own words, was the greatest love of her life, and after having endured the impertinence of judicial interrogators and especially that of journalists and photographers, Tina Modotti has returned to her former life; that is, to her work as a photographer, searching for comfort in the work waiting for her in her studio. We found her at home, number 31, busy and absorbed in looking through negatives. Dressed modestly and with her face practically without makeup, her lustrous hair pulled back, she went from one side of the room to the other, picking up a test tube here, fixing a negative there. She excused herself for not seeing to us properly, but for her those were intense moments in her work and she was driven to finish a delicate job. On leaving the residence, with its noticeable bohemian atmosphere, we were informed that Tina Modotti had told a lawyer to take legal action against a morning newspaper for having libeled her reputation when describing her as a woman of the street. Tina will present to the judge photographs in which she appeared nude in order to prove that they were not pornographic shots but rather artistic studies.

Part One

THE YOUNG

REVOLUTIONARY

One

Assunta Adelaide Luigia Modotti was born in Udine, Italy, on August 17, 1896, the second of six children. Her father, Giuseppe, supported his large family by working as a mason, and his work often took him to Austria for long periods when he was unable to find work in nearby Friuli. The six children helped their mother when they could, doing odd jobs, until their father took them with him to Austria. A man of socialist ideas, Giuseppe Modotti participated in demonstrations and attended meetings, and among Tina's most vivid childhood memories was the traditional May Day demonstration: a sea of heads and red flags, seen from her father's shoulders.

When the Modottis returned to Udine, Tina was nine years old. Her main concerns were still the same: to find food for dinner and firewood to warm their pitiful home. She left school after third grade and began to help with the occasional work her mother could find as a dressmaker. When she was twelve years old she was hired by the Raiser silk factory in the suburbs of Udine. Her sister Yolanda remembered her, from that point on, as having a sad face and a resigned look, the only one who never complained about the lack of food or the cold.

It was at this time that Giuseppe Modotti decided to venture to the United States, a common decision at the turn of the century for Italian lower-class workingmen. He arrived in San Francisco with his firstborn, Mercedes, and accepted whatever work he could get so that he would be able to send enough money to the rest of his family for their future trip. Tina did not wait long, and in 1913, seventeen years old and alone, she left on a cargo ship packed with emigrants. After only one week in San Francisco, she found work in a textile factory. All around her the great labor movements of the era were growing in size and strength. The Industrial Workers of the World (IWW or Wobblies) were organizing resistance to armed employers' groups and calling strikes in which thousands of workers participated. Los Angeles and San Francisco had become strongholds for the opposition against repressive violence. A wave of strikes rose, starting in the textile mills of Massachusetts and spreading throughout the country.

San Francisco, moreover, was home to many artistic and cultural activities that distinguished it from any other American city. Not founded by Anglo-Saxon Protestants, San Francisco developed as a city without Puritan influences, much like the great European cities that favored radical innovations and a healthy indifference toward conventional morality.

Modotti began to frequent workers' circles and theater groups in the Italian district of San Francisco. She soon left the factory, supporting herself by working at home as a dressmaker. This allowed her more time to dedicate to the small amateur theater company, in which she stood out from others because of the passion she conveyed while acting. On stage she seemed to become transformed, and the contrast was even more noticeable given her shy, taciturn character, shrouded in the impalpable veil of gloom that always surrounded her.

The responsibility she felt toward her family did not prevent her from spending every minute of her free time attending debates, meetings, and exhibitions in a progressive spiral of initiatives and new knowledge. Restlessness and the need for independence led her to become involved in everything without ever committing herself entirely to anything. Everything interested Modotti, but nothing seemed to satisfy her. The theater continued to lure her, but no more so than anything else. She felt the need to overcome the ghetto wall, to make the jump that would finally free her from a life consisting of the thousands of precarious jobs she had to take in order to survive, and which allowed her only fragments of passion.

At the Pan-Pacific International Exhibition, Tina met the painter and poet Roubaix de l'Abrie Richey, known to all as Robo. Originally from Quebec, he was residing at that time in Los Angeles. Tall and very thin, with long hair, a dark mustache, and dark eyes, Robo had a look about him as if he were lost in an imaginary world that excluded even his closest friends. He fell in love with Modotti's sad beauty and her indecipherable character, and he saw in her the same vague subtle malaise that made him feel like a stranger to life.

Two years went by before Modotti made the decision to distance herself from the stagnant, protective microcosm of San Francisco's Italian neighborhood. Marrying Robo was a way for her to leave it behind. She liked Robo and perhaps could even have grown to love him if only she could have overcome the invisible wall of emptiness that he put up between himself and the world, if only she could have broken the cocoon into which he retreated every time he felt he might get hurt.

In their enormous house in Los Angeles, Modotti continued to work as a dressmaker, but now economic freedom allowed her to create patterns and let her fantasy run wild cutting fabrics and combining colors. Robo's studio was a gathering place for radical artists and writers, a perennial coming and going of personalities searching for something they felt was missing from their lives but which they could not define.

The postwar years in Los Angeles were an exaggeration of contrasts, a short circuit from conservatism to the frenetic search for new values. Robo's garden served as the setting for heated discussions about socialism and the revolution, as well as sexual freedom and individual independence as fundamental requirements for political and artistic expression. Enthusiastic attacks on prevailing morals combined with a curiosity about Eastern philosophies and the limits of perception; Marxist theories and a fascination with anarchical ideas now replaced the interest in psychoanalysis and the crisis of Christianity. For them, changing the world meant not only rejecting a power or a government, but above all transforming themselves and putting into practice what they believed. Exclusive relationships, the very idea of couples, crumbled in the face of their ideology.

Modotti was no longer content to spend her entire day with fabrics and a sewing machine. She was now conscious of her own beauty and the fascination it caused in all who were near her. The environment around her intensified her need to make her mark as an individual, and she decided to exploit her experience in the theater in order to realize a long-held dream. Hollywood was at her doorstep, and every day screen tests launched new stars. Modotti was surprised at how easily the doors opened for her in the mecca of film. In part she may have owed this to Rodolfo Valentino, whose inordinate success had caused producers to see a guaranteed source of income in any "Italian beauty." At first she put all her energy into that unique method of performing, without the power of a script or words, imagining that the directors and producers of silent film would notice her dramatic expression and her self-assurance on stage. But in fact it was always her figure that made the biggest impression in her screen tests. She was dressed as a Gypsy and as an odalisque, and was offered roles as a femme fatale and a voluptuous lover. In 1920 she made several films; in one of them she appeared nude, wrapped in a lace veil that left one breast exposed. "Flexible and curvaceous, her walk is slow and harmonious, her eyes an ardent black," she was described at the time. And in the program for *The Tiger's Coat*, the words "the exotic charm of Tina Modotti" were underlined. She played similar roles in *Riding with Death* and *I Can Explain*, but her ambition was not sufficient to lead her to accept other offers of scripts written for her type. The movies would be a parenthesis in her life. Although she did not regret this period, she would later prefer to forget it. The rare times she did watch one of her films, it was to laugh about it with her friends.

The year 1920 was also the one in which Modotti's mother moved to San Francisco with the other children, Benvenuto, Giuseppe, and Yolanda. Only Valentina remained behind in Udine. In 1917 she had been involved with a soldier and as a result had had a son, Tullio. When the man returned to the front, she heard nothing more from him.

Valentina decided to stay in Italy after the war ended, perhaps hoping that one day the father of her child would return.

Once Modotti left acting, she felt the need to find other expressive outlets for her creative instinct. Photography was still a young art form whose possibilities were as yet unexplored. Among the regulars at Robo's studio was Edward Weston, who was regarded as a master of the image; his renown was such that he could afford to turn down commissions. Weston met Modotti at a critical time in his life. Unable to bear routine work and suffocated by family responsibilities, he was full of worry and indecision. He was tempted by the idea of leaving his wife and children to venture south, drawn by the idea of postrevolutionary Mexico. In the meantime, he poured his heart out to his closest friends, who saw his extravagant character often reach a neurotic level. But he also had a magnetic energy, a charisma undoubtedly helped by being the most famous and widely understood of the tight circle of artists surrounding Robo.

Modotti became excited by Weston's photographic techniques, posed for him, and at the same time asked questions, studied, and observed, missing not a single word during the days she spent with him. The eagerness with which she took on every activity conquered Weston's extreme sensibility. Not only for her beauty but also for the natural enthusiasm she exuded, he fell in love with her so completely that for a few days he forgot everything else. His feelings of guilt with respect to Robo, whom he considered one of his best friends, vanished in the spasmodic expectation of every new encounter. At first they behaved as secret lovers, but it became impossible for either one to hide the evidence of their love. Only a few hours of separation were enough to spark off an exchange of frantic letters written with the passion characteristic of their first few days together. What was once restlessness in Modotti had now become an all-consuming desire. She wrote to Weston in April 1921:

> One night after—all day I have been intoxicated with the memory of last night and overwhelmed with the beauty and madness of it . . . How can I wait until we meet again! Once more I have been reading your letter and as at every other time my eyes are full of tears—I never realized before

*that a letter—a mere sheet of paper—could be such a spirited thing—
could emanate so much feeling—you gave a soul to it! Oh! If I could be
with you now at this hour I love so much, I would try to tell you how
much beauty has been added to my life lately! When may I come over? I
am waiting for your call . . . I need but to close my eyes to find myself not
once more but still near you in that beloved darkness—with the flavor of
wine yet on my lips and the impression of your mouth on mine. Oh how
wonderful to recall every moment of our hours together—fondle them
and gently carry them in me like frail and precious dreams—and now
while I write to you—from my still quivering senses rises an ardent desire
to again kiss your eyes and mouth.*

Her relationship with Robo seemed to dissolve in shadows whose out-
lines became more and more vague. Robo realized what was going on,
but his passive nature and his custom of living on the margin of things,
of touching on them without ever involving himself in them, led him to
live apart from the world. In Weston, Modotti found the exact opposite:
his nonconformist impulsiveness, the contrast between his gentle way of
speaking and his stormy outbursts when referring to subjects that excited
him, and his possessiveness of her. She was twenty-five and he, thirty-
four. The shy, quiet figure of Robo began to fade away, becoming less
substantial in comparison to the energy of a man accustomed to snatch-
ing even the smallest concession from life.

After losing his mother at the age of five, Edward Weston grew up in
the Midwest with his older sister and his father, who gave him a Bulls-
Eye camera on his sixteenth birthday. His decision to embark on the precarious career of traveling photographer took him to Chicago, and from
there to Nevada and California, as he followed the railroad, documenting
its workers. Like Modotti, he experienced the daily struggle against
poverty firsthand, and success came only after years of deprivation and a
stubborn faith in photographic art. But when the time came to reap the
rewards, Weston strongly rejected the commercial photographs that
magazines in several countries were requesting.

His marriage to Flora May Chandler, a woman who had been educated in the traditional manner and whose ideas were completely op-

posed to his, ended up being a purely practical arrangement for the sake of their four children. Weston's relationships with other women were a symptom of his growing dissatisfaction: They lasted only days or weeks but contributed to destroying his marriage with Flora. However, his guilt over his children, whom he adored, prevented him from taking the decisive step toward the journey that he now saw as his only chance for artistic renewal.

Physical attraction was surely the catalyst for Modotti, but her relationship with Weston also gave her the chance to dominate an expressive medium that immediately captivated her and to which she dedicated her entire being. Through photography she discovered the outlet for feelings that until then she had only sensed without ever managing to take hold of.

Robo returned once and for all to the solitude in which, deep down, he had always lived. Withdrawal from the material nature of things was his existential nature. While others continued to include him in their artistic projects, he told Modotti of his decision to leave for Mexico at year's end, and he dedicated one final poem to her: "Tina is red like wine, so precious that it must be left to age delicately so it may become even more precious."

Mexico, surprisingly, seemed to transform Robo. In the letters he wrote to Weston there emerged a new figure, that of a passionate man full of interest who had finally managed to touch and seize what was going on around him. He defined Mexico as a "land of extremes" and described it as a paradise for creativity:

> There is little that is devoid of beauty. There is for me more poetry in one lone serape-enshrouded figure leaning in the door of the pulque shop at twilight or a bronzen daughter of the Aztecs nursing her child in a church than could be found in Los Angeles in the next ten years . . . Can you imagine an art school where every thing is free to everyone— Mexicans and foreigners alike—tuition-board-room-paint-canvas-models-all free—No entrance examination—If one will study that is the only requirement. After ten years of war and unrest it is wonderful to see what is being done here.

In his descriptions of landscapes, of faces, and of nature that is violent and at the same time gentle and tormented, Robo conveyed new emotions. He tried to persuade Weston to join him, and he did so with sincere enthusiasm and with the certainty that his art could not miss an opportunity like that. He had already agreed with Modotti that they would see each other again down in Mexico, and he vibrated with the thought of showing them both all that he was living. He alluded only briefly to the relationship that had begun with Modotti, as if wanting to assure his friend that nothing could or should change the affection that bonded them: "Believe me, I am still, as always, your friend Robo."

A few days later, on February 9, 1922, Robo suddenly came down with a very high fever, probably due to smallpox, and died. At that moment Modotti was crossing the border, headed for Mexico City.

Two

A boy who has disappeared from a world to which he never belonged. A boy with eyes clouded by dreams, filled with an uncertainty that is eternally present in souls so sensitive as to perceive it . . .

Modotti added those words to the book in which she was compiling everything that Robo had written, in memory of a poet with a transient look who felt unhappy among people but who was incapable of hurting anyone, preferring to hide in the shadows so as not to reveal his incurable melancholy.

The first place Modotti visited when she arrived in Mexico City was the Panteón de Dolores, the immense cemetery located on the western outskirts of the capital. She learned of Robo's death in a telegram given to her on the train, and she now had to take charge of all the preparations regarding his funeral. Friends of the young artist gathered around Modotti, even those whom he had known only a few weeks. Now alone in Mexico, Modotti was drawn to the convulsive rhythms of the barely revived country and to the fervor with which everyone was helping to built a utopian society. Ricardo Gómez Robledo, director of the Ministry of Fine Arts and a regular at Robo's studio, served as her guide to the series of initiatives that had created a climate of electrifying euphoria in the city. Artists from all disciplines returned from the ranks of the guerrilla armies or from exile in Europe, where they had witnessed the destruction caused by war. Setting their rifles aside, they created improvised schools and street workshops; farmers painted their tractors and reapers bright colors; the walls of buildings, barracks, churches, and universities were covered with endless murals. An atmosphere of renewed excitement and liberated energy permeated the city, and everything seemed on the verge of beginning, without limits or boundaries.

Álvaro Obregón had become president, and he entrusted the secretaryship of the Ministry of Education to José Vasconcelos, who had recently returned from five years in exile. Vasconcelos believed strongly in the involvement of artists in all aspects of social life, and he abolished all forms of censorship and ideological pressure. Mexico City became the epicenter of the avant-garde from every corner of the world.

Modotti knew at once that she could not return to the superficial and luxurious life of Los Angeles. In Mexico she felt life throbbing with the same frenzy she had noticed inside herself years before—the restlessness that had been repressed for so long inside an enclosed house and garden, with a few chosen ones, but whose natural destiny was the street, meeting people, exchanging emotions, and living fully without wasting a single second and without looking back.

She had brought some of Weston's photos with her to Mexico. As she began to show them she was surprised by the unexpected interest they generated. Mexican artists were now discovering the expressive power of photography, and they no longer regarded it as merely a technical craft. An exhibition was held, and an impressive number of people gathered to view Weston's work. Modotti felt alive with renewed spirit.

But once again death intervened, interrupting the beginning of her passionate endeavor. In March 1922 Modotti's father died in San Francisco, and she returned to the United States.

· · ·

Modotti spent more than a month with her family, absorbed once again by the ties from which she had temporarily fled. The loss of Robo and her father in the course of two months caused her to feel regretful and indecisive. She avoided Weston and found a calming refuge for her confused feelings in her mother's home. But photography managed slowly to regain her interest, leading her to get back in touch with Johan Hagemeyer, a photographer and intellectual anarchist, as well as a musician and close friend of Weston. Modotti had met Hagemeyer in August 1921, and in one of her letters from September of that same year there is the sense that he had awakened an extraordinary interest in her.

> *I have written you about a dozen letters in my mind but never have I been able to put them into written form. Not for lack of thoughts—instead—the impressions left to me of the afternoon spent with you were so many and so deep they overwhelmed my mind. But here I am making a brave effort to express all I feel, full-well knowing it is futile—for not even to myself can I clearly answer why I suppressed the great desire I had to call on you once more. Was it power of will? Or was it cowardice? Maybe the same spirit moved me then, what moved Oscar Wilde to write this paradox. "There are only two tragedies in this world; one consists in not obtaining that which you desire; the other consists in obtaining it." The last one is the worst—the last is a real tragedy. And so I left without satisfying my desire of listening once more to Pergolesi's* Niña *in your company.*

Hagemeyer had given her that record, one of the lesser-known works of Pergolesi. For Modotti it seemed to have been the ideal background music in those moments when she felt nostalgia for something undefinable, the symptom of something she realized was missing but could not pinpoint. She wrote to him again in the spring of 1922:

> *I hesitated long whether to get in touch with you or not for I had made it my programme before coming here not to see anyone outside of my family. But the other day—finding myself alone—an uncontrollable desire came upon me to hear* Niña *again. And so I did—and as I listened to it the agitated life of these past few months came back to me with all the il-*

lusion of reality—a certain afternoon when for the first time that soul-
torturing music took hold of me and left me a little sadder perhaps but
with a richer soul. And because of all this I feel the desire to spend the af-
ternoon with you—can the first ever be duplicated? I fear not—but Niña
at least will be the same. Can you drop me a card and let me know when
I can call you? I will remain here until Easter—fond as I am of this
place—yet I am anxious to leave it—it holds too many memories for
me—here I live constantly in the past, and "Life," said George Moore, "is
beautiful at the moment, but sad when we look back." For me life is al-
ways sad—for even in the present moment I feel the past. Mine must be a
spirit of decadence, and by living here I only give vent to it—but yet—I
feel that only by living in the past can we [avenge] ourselves on nature—
I wonder how you feel about all this—perhaps we can talk it over.

Modotti went back to using her camera, if only sporadically, and her
closeness to Hagemeyer stimulated her to work more intensely. She began to see more of Weston again, and soon they resumed their relationship with the same level of intensity that it had prior to Robo's death, but
this time it was he who felt the weight of family responsibilities. Modotti
sympathized with Weston's turmoil and his reluctance to leave his children; but her desire to go to Mexico led her to make a final decision. Weston was intrigued by all that she had told him about her enthusiasm for
her work that had been stirred up in Mexico, but he continued to post-
pone his trip, obsessed by economic concerns and by the impossibility of
turning down jobs being offered to him in several U.S. cities.

By October a break in their relationship seemed inevitable. Modotti
wrote:

Good-bye—good-bye Edward—may you attain all you deserve—but is
that possible—you give so much—how can "Life" ever pay you back? I
can only send a few rose petals and a kiss.

The separation lasted a few months, and during this time Modotti
continued to ask mutual friends for news of Weston. Their bond had not
been broken, and he, so as not to lose her, ended up taking the much
postponed step. Once he had regained confidence in his work, thanks to
an exhibition in New York, Weston left his wife, taking with him his

thirteen-year-old son, Chandler. On July 30, 1923, Weston, Modotti, and Chandler boarded the *Colima*, headed for Manzanillo.

After what seemed like an interminable trip by train through the states of Colima, Jalisco, Guanajuato, Querétaro, and Hidalgo, practically an initiation rite that overwhelms the eyes, given the enormity of the country, the three arrived in Mexico City and rented a big house in Tacubaya, a suburb that at that time had not yet been absorbed by the city. The house had ten rooms that opened onto an interior patio, high ceilings, arched windows, thick walls, and a garden that was an explosion of colors. The rooftop had a view of the bell tower of the cathedral located in the Zócalo in Mexico City and the immense valley dominated by the two volcanoes, the majestic Popocatépetl and Iztaccíhuatl, called "the sleeping woman" because of its shape.

Unlike many North Americans who went to Mexico to "aid" the revolution or to study the Aztec and Mayan cultures, Modotti and Weston immersed themselves in the life of the country. They immediately found themselves in contact with the myriad people who were dedicating their energy to the affirmation of the new values of the "revived Mexico." They met Diego Rivera, who for a few years would be inseparable from their group, David Alfaro Siqueiros, and José Clemente Orozco. Tina saw Xavier Guerrero again, whom she had met in Los Angeles at one of his exhibitions and who was now working on the murals at Chapingo with Rivera and Siqueiros.

The Mexican artistic movement had manifested itself as a cultural rebellion before the political and social rebellion had taken shape. Orozco had reunited a small group of art students to initiate the insurrection against Huerta's dictatorship, and in 1919 an assembly of artists was formed that would proclaim the indissoluble union between cultural expression and armed revolution. Rivera had spent some time in Paris during the Cubist period and there he had met Picasso, Klee, Braque, and Matisse, and later travelled to Italy to study frescos, Byzantine mosaics, and Etruscan artifacts, finding in the latter an affinity with the ancient indigenous art of Mexico. After serving as a cavalry officer in the Army of Carranza, Siqueiros had taken several trips through Europe, publishing a manifesto on his conception of mural painting in Barcelona in 1921. Once back in Mexico, he founded the Revolutionary Syndicate of Techni-

cal Workers, Painters, and Sculptors, and in *El Machete*, the organization's newspaper, he praised the efforts being made to squelch the old political and artistic conceptions.

Art became a collective expression, rejecting the commercialization of
the canvas in the name of murals, which stood as public property. The
aesthetic goal was to socialize creativity and destroy bourgeois individualism. Everything took place in the open air, in improvised spaces, or in
spaces wrested from the old institutions. Activities combined and over-
lapped; while some painted, others played music, taught, or debated.
The intensity of frenzied stimuli led Modotti to surrender herself completely to the schools, parks, gardens, archaeological expeditions, meetings and to groups presenting petitions and proposals. But she also threw
herself into the unending parties, dancing, drinking, and tireless interac-
tion with people. She served as a guide to Weston, who immersed himself
in everything with overwhelming wonder. His ability to learn languages
quickly and his affinity with all that was Latin, something that was immediately obvious to Mexicans, soon made him a public figure.

They left their house in Tacubaya, which they considered too far from
the pulsating center of the city, and moved to Lucerna Street in the central Colonía Juarez. In just a few months their apartment would become a
reference point of artistic and cultural life. Among the regulars on lively
nights were writers Juan de la Cabada and Anita Brenner, the painter Jean
Charlot, the photographer Manuel Álvarez Bravo, Rivera's wife, Lupe
Marín, and her brother Federico Marín, along with José Vasconcelos and
the muralists who had already been coming to the residence.

One of the more enigmatic figures in the group, due to his mysterious
past, was a German-speaking writer, Bruno Traven. Of unknown nation-
ality, he had been living in Mexico since 1920, and although he displayed
a natural friendship with Tina and Weston, he never confided his true
identity to them. And, with regard to certain activities, Traven would
continue to be a mystery that would never be completely deciphered.
Some believe he was an Austrian whose name was Berick Torsvan, but
others say he was born in Chicago, perhaps in 1890, and grew up in Central Europe. Attracted by anarchist ideals, he participated in the Munich
rebellion in 1918 and was later hunted by the police for his subversive
activities. Having arrived in Mexico after a long underground journey

through several countries, Traven proved to be one of the few foreigners capable of capturing and assimilating the Mexican spirit. Until his final days, he avoided appearing in public, to such an extent that when the young John Huston decided to make a movie based on Traven's novel *The Treasure of the Sierra Madre*, the author wrote him saying that he could not collaborate with him on the adaptation, but assured him that someone close to him would go as his representative. After several weeks on the set, Traven's "emissary" disappeared into thin air, and not until many years later did Huston discover that he had been dealing with the author himself, who had shown great skill in not appearing in any of the photographs taken during the filming of the movie.

In his photos of the time, Weston reveals what the group themselves defined as a "bohemian atmosphere," like the one in which Jean Charlot is absorbed in writing on Modotti's bare back. Weston's jealousy was quickly apparent. His fears were confirmed by Lupe Marín, who publicly accused Modotti of being her husband, Diego's, lover.

Modotti's charm gave rise to delirious behavior at times. Exaggeration was the norm during that era of confusion, and she herself did not seem overly surprised when one of the many artists she had met at a party, completely in love with and rejected by her, returned with a gun begging her to kill him. Federico Marín described her as "a mysterious beauty, without any trace of vulgarity. . . . Not happy but rather austere, terribly austere. Neither melancholy nor tragic, but there are men who fall madly in love with her, and some have gone as far as to commit suicide."

In his memoirs, written many years later, Vasconcelos also described Modotti as a woman capable of driving men to the point of madness. "With her sculptural and depraved beauty, she held the group together by a common desire but at the same time divided it by causing vicious rivalries." Vasconcelos didn't stop at this, going on to say that the death of Gómez Robelo, on August 6, 1924, could also be attributed to his unrequited love for Modotti. "That unhealthy passion made him thin and drugged his soul . . . until he died, devoured by desire."

Torn between the sexual freedom he defended and his most intimate instincts, Weston jotted succinctly in his diary, "Next time it will be better for me to look for a woman who is ugly as the devil."

•   •   •

These were the years in which Mexican culture was being lashed by the "electropoetic discharges" of the Movimiento Estridentista, and it was at this time that Tina met Germán List Arzubide, a poet and one of the movement's founders. With her Korona, more manageable than the Graflex used by Weston, Modotti took some photographs of the young poet that emphasized, even more than his works, the torment of destructive passions stirring inside him.

When List Arzubide and Modotti met at the Café de Nadie on Jalisco Avenue they were, unavoidably, mutually awed. She was experimenting at the time with photographic techniques involving overexposure, achieving effects that Álvarez Bravo would later define as a "crystal impression," and some of her works were immediately recognized as "Estridentista photographs." Several photos signed by Modotti appeared in the movement's magazines, such as images of the symmetry of superimposed electric poles, the rows of cables fleeing toward the sky, and the strange geometric patterns of steps in a stadium.

Like European Futurism, Estridentism was characterized by the sharp, exasperated stroke in the graphic arts and by plastic dynamism in painting, an interest in machines, especially planes, and, naturally, the declaration of war on "pastism." But unlike Futurism, Estridentista poets used more irony and vicious sarcasm, including comic provocation, than the automatic writing of "free words." Estridentista poetry was "music of ideas," which exalted the contrast between dark notes and bright notes, comparing the sound of words with those of the saxophone and jazz percussion. Radio was regarded as the ideal medium for poetic diffusion, so much so that Estridentista publications were not defined as "organs" of the movement but rather as "irradiations." As one of their manifestos declared:

It's time for the seven-league boots, time for the winged horse: we perfume ourselves with gasoline and we know the madness of the sun. We fly in an airplane over heads pained by boredom, we sing with the power of the propeller that defies the laws of gravity. We are Estridentistas, and we cast stones at the houses crammed full of furniture aged by silence, where the dust consumes the movement of light. The flies won't leave their writing on our documents, because after they are read they will only be used for wrapping sugar. And we, bristling with microscopic rays, will go on inflicting discharges on those sick with indolence.

Diego Rivera also approached the Estridentistas, although without adhering to their manifesto. The movement considered Rivera's mural in the Ministry of Education to be an example of painting that was very close to their view of art. But in the plastic arts it was Germán Cueto who embodied the movement's ideas. Defining himself as a "designer," Cueto created the model "Estridentistas in the Year 1975," a futuristic vision of an Estridentista city that was ideally to be built in Jalapa, the capital of Veracruz. Cueto lived on the top floor of a half-abandoned building that was chosen as the movement's headquarters. On the door was a sign that read:

GERMAN CUETO—DESIGNS. Using our incongruous instruments we will tell you what you are feeling. We know the quadrature of space. Our measurements are based on the fourth dimension. We listen to the heart of infinity. Do you want to be a hero? We know the map of the future, we can suggest a course for future events. Come see us. Free advice for those lacking in imagination.

The Estridentistas attacked the paralysis of academia and ridiculed critics who were "bilious, corroded by the purulent wounds of the plague-stricken and dying literary has-beens." They declared themselves to be the natural children of the Mexican revolution, but they warned that revolutions must be cut off in time to prevent them from becoming reactionary. They vehemently attacked the old masters from different creative and cultural fields, accusing them of having been converted by Porfiristas (followers of Mexican president Porfirio Díaz) into henchmen of the dictator Victoriano Huerta, to the point of falsely embracing the revolution to obtain government posts. This caused the Estridentistas to be ostracized from the publishing world tied to universities and ministries, of which the ex-Porfiristas had skillfully made themselves an integral part. However, they received the support of the old poet Rafael López, who in their name rejected the official invitation to enter the academy of the greatest men of letters.

"We will extinguish the sun with a huge hat," read one headline in
Horizonte, a magazine run by List Arzubide and in whose pages Modotti's photographs received an enthusiastic reception. She was immediately swept up in the parties of the Estridentistas, where the subversive
power of laughter was praised and new collective vitality was drawn for
successive provocations.

> The Estridentistas hold their dances on the fifth floor of a cluster of
> apartments decorated with clotheslines and under the protection of the
> surrounding mountains, strict moral guardians of our parties. Girls from
> the movies, with supershort hair, plunging necklines, and their legs open
> wide, fill the shabby little patio, dressed like moon princesses. And down
> there, inside the cage, the musicians break out in a sudden rebellion: The
> music explodes like magnesium, and we all begin to bob about desper-
> ately, afraid to sink in the night in this drunken boat, full of streamers of
> happiness that the music carries away.

For the Estridentistas, liberation from the old cultural dogmas could
only move forward together with political renewal and the alteration of
social customs, not to mention sexual and personal relationships. It was
the same path that Modotti had already been traveling for several years.
She was still attracting attention for her "obscure beauty, streaked with a
sadness that contrasts with an energy that infects whoever is near her,"
but also for her originality in dress: She almost always wore blue jeans,
completely uncommon for women of her time.

And all the while Weston seemed torn between allowing himself to be
dragged along and trying to hold her back. He felt the aesthetic fascination of the Movimiento Estridentista for a time, and one of his photographs even appeared on the cover of *Irradiador*, the magazine run by
Maples Arec. In another of his many published photos, part of a woman's
face can be seen emerging from beneath a geometric composition. The
face resembles Modotti's, and she probably posed for the image, which
Weston titled *Lo Incógnito* (the unknown).

Three

By this time Modotti was beginning to assert her independence as a photographer. She was no longer Weston's assistant, limiting herself to imitating his techniques and his themes. She traveled around the city taking photos with her Korona. Alone she went to neighboring states in search of faces, images that captured a moment in life that patient studio experimentation could not express, and she developed the negatives herself, perfecting certain techniques to complete each job. Weston was amazed by her progress, but he increasingly sensed a feeling of remoteness that he was not able to overcome: "The night before we had been alone—so seldom happens now. She called me to her room and our lips met for the first time since New Year's Eve. Then the doorbell rang . . . our mood was gone."

In May 1924, two months shy of the first anniversary of their "union," they moved to a new house in Colonia Roma on Veracruz Avenue. And so, in late July, Weston and Modotti got dressed in the most conventional clothing they owned and went to the first photographer's studio they could find downtown, saying they wanted to commemorate their "marriage." Against a backdrop that resembled the interior of a church, they struck a serious pose, and with reason: He was seated with what could be a Bible on his lap and she was standing, with one hand on the shoulder of her "husband" and a bouquet of roses in the other. They repeated the joke, against a background of blurred trees and bushes, holding hands in a boring pose. Edward is looking at her and there is a certain restlessness in his look, almost a request for approval. She, on the other hand, is staring directly at the lens, which probably caught her unaware as she sighed, half resigned and half amused.

Modotti's first exhibition was in 1924, when she showed her photos at a group show at the Palacio de Minería. The reception was positive, and Weston, who helped her with her most recent works, stated, "Tina's photos lose nothing next to mine. They represent her personal expression." The critics, now appreciating her work, no longer regarded her as a mere student of Weston and emphasized the originality of her expressive exploration.

Her first commissioned job was to illustrate a book on Mexico by Anita Brenner with her photos, and the magazine *Forma*, edited by Gabriel Fernández Ledesma, began to publish her work. Nevertheless, the more recognition she earned in the field of book illustrating, the more she felt the need to unify her work with what was going on around her. Her interest in social problems transformed into political passion, and her doubts about the relationship between art and her militant commitment increased. Experimentation and research were no longer enough for her. Modotti became convinced that photography too, *especially* photography, must express something beyond aesthetic formalism, which was by that time turning toward rarefaction, toward pure abstraction. She felt that she must influence reality by representing its most controversial aspects, capturing its malaise, and exalting the power of rebellion wherever it appeared.

In the summer of 1924 she returned briefly to the theater, where she accepted a melodramatic role in the Mexican translation of *Le Chauve-Souris*. On opening night, September 17, Modotti took the stage demonstrating "great command and extreme discretion," in the words of Weston, who would tell her that night that he thought the theater to be the most appropriate place for her. But this would only be a temporary passion. After the run of performances was over, she left the stage, this time for good.

By now differences between Modotti and Weston were becoming more pronounced. Their relationship, already damaged by neglect and Weston's jealousy, was also now suffering from the contrasts of two differing artistic conceptions that verged on conflict. Almost as if he knew what was to come, Weston decided to do a long series of portraits of Modotti, as if wanting to capture her face before their imminent separation.

> The new head of Tina is printed. Along with Lupe's head it is the best I have done in Mexico, perhaps the best I have done at all. But while Lupe's is heroic, this head of Tina is noble, majestic, exalted; the face of a woman who has suffered, known death and disillusion, who has sold herself to rich men and given herself to poor, whose childhood knew privation and hard work, whose maturity will bring together the bittersweet experience of one who has lived life fully, deeply, and unafraid.

She also posed for him nude. Weston always photographed her lying on the ground with her eyes closed and her body arched, barely grazing the ground. Taken on the terrace in the middle of the day, these photos transmitted a sensation of delicacy in relief, of a skin that absorbed and reflected the heat of the sun. No other image of Modotti represented so deeply her relationship with Mexico: the nature of transgression, the sensual abandon illuminated by the sun, without shadows, a physicality that emanated tenderness and sadness. It was an era that was coming to an end. In the ensuing years, she would no longer be able to see Mexico as she had during those unique and unrepeatable days.

Modotti was gaining security, a command of the expressive medium, and although she continued to live frugally, she managed to support herself by taking portraits and selling her photos to magazines. Next to her, almost by some strange alchemy of communicating vessels, Weston began, little by little, to feel insecure and troubled by dissatisfaction in spite of his success in Mexico, and he felt a growing and imperative need to see his other children again. Only by returning to Glendale would he be able to free himself from the now obvious anguish that had overcome him. But Chandler had adjusted to the environment in such a way that he did not share his father's anxiety at all. When Weston decided to leave the house on Veracruz Avenue, his fourteen-year-old son was tempted to stay with Modotti. Only a few days prior to his father's departure did he decide to leave and go see his mother again.

This separation was not definitive. Weston was sure that he would return, although he did not know when. Modotti did not say good-bye to him, but she was aware that the real distance between them was not due to the thousands of kilometers separating Mexico City from California. Something had changed in their mutual feelings, and the more she embraced the social aspects of the reality that surrounded her, the more he closed himself up inside a pessimistic individualism.

In late December 1924, Weston returned to the United States. Modotti gave him a letter before his departure.

What is the use of words between Edward and [me]? He knows me and I know him and we both have faith in each other. And that to me, Edward, seems the most precious gain we have acquired from each other—the faith in each other. I will be a good girl while you are gone, Edward—I will work hard and that for two reasons—that you may be proud of me and that the time of our separation may move more swiftly. Edward— beloved—thank you—whatever comes.

She entered a transitional period. Without Weston her political interest lost a kind of protective barrier formed by his rejection of ideologies. Modotti was able to devote herself completely to her photography, without having to endure the influence of Weston's possessiveness, but she was drawn by the climate of major and rapid change that was disrupting Mexico and the world. She felt that she could not just watch what was happening from behind the lens. She recognized her irresistible need to oppose with an even greater commitment the forces that were shattering the achievements of the revolution. More than any other Latin American country, Mexico came under attack from the colonialism of the Monroe Doctrine, which was transforming Central America into the backyard of the United States. In Mexico, "America for Americans" meant the control of resources, the most important of these being oil, and the holding of elections that favored candidates who bowed to the desires of Washington. The Soviet utopia nourished Latin American hopes, but Moscow was far away, shrouded in a legend that reached out from the other hemisphere while, only a few kilometers away, on the other side of the Río Bravo, fervent efforts were being made to eliminate any remainder of the legacy of Francisco Villa and Emiliano Zapata.

In a letter from Modotti to Weston dated July 7, 1925, a deep internal confusion can be detected, as well as her doubts about what was really worth doing in this difficult situation:

> *I have not been very "creative," Edward—less than a print a month— that is terrible! And yet it is not lack of interest so much as lack of discipline and power of execution . . . speaking of my personal self—I cannot—as you once proposed to me—solve the problems of my life by losing myself in the problem of art—not only I cannot do that but I even feel that the problem of life hinders my problem of art.*

Tina continued her association with Diego Rivera, who was a militant member of the Mexican Communist Party, and she met Vladimir Mayakovski, who had also been lured to the Mexican capital by its artistic and political unrest. Tina took several photographs of the Russian poet, some of which were published in *El Universal Ilustrado*, and she accompanied him on his long walks through the colonial center of the city and to the receptions organized in his honor by the Soviet Embassy.

In the meantime her friendship with Xavier Guerrero, who was experiencing a similar decline in interest in the work of the pure muralist vis-à-vis total revolutionary militancy, was intensifying. Time seemed to pass more quickly each day, and life in the Mexican capital allowed less and less room for those who aspired to perform two activities simultaneously. Guerrero feared, even before Modotti did, that the time he devoted to painting was undeniably inhibiting his participation in the construction of the New World. Moreover, as a Mexican, he felt he had to defend the little that remained of a revolution reabsorbed by bureaucracy and divided by foreign financial partnerships. Modotti was fascinated by

Guerrero's unbreakable, granitelike faith, by his Indian-appearing face that embodied millennia of vexations and humiliations, by his long silences that emanated ancient wisdom. The rare times he spoke, he did so in a calm voice that drove away doubts and confirmed certainties. Guerrero's influence on Modotti would be a determining factor in the decisions she would make in the tragic years to come.

Four

Weston returned to Mexico in August 1925 with his fourteen-year-old son Brett. The trip was inspired in part by an exhibition of his and Modotti's photographs in Guadalajara. Weston and Modotti stayed ten days in the capital city of Jalisco, home of the most deeply rooted Mexican traditions and the region that produced all the country's tequila. Their reunion seemed to renew the passion they once had, despite the fact that the exhibition was not as successful with the public as they had hoped. Local newspaper critics, on the other hand, gave the event wide coverage. The introduction to an interview given by Modotti read, "She appeared, self-confident, wearing a high-necked silk blouse and a man's tie, which contrasted with her very straight North American–style skirt."

On returning to Mexico City, they immersed themselves once again in the unbridled rhythm of parties, dances, and reunions with old and new friends until dawn, and their house was once again filled with people coming and going just like the previous year, as if they had picked up exactly where they had left off. And inevitably Weston's jealousy resurfaced. In his diary he wrote of an uncontrollable aversion toward a certain "Doctor M." who was displaying genuine adoration for Modotti. He was referring to a German, Leo M. Matthias, who in 1926 would write a book on Mexico that began with his thanking both Tina and Weston, and in which, among other things, he stated, "Tina is a woman of average height and extraordinary beauty. Her face, its tragic expression, reminds me of Eleonora Duse. . . . If only I had been able to win her away from Weston, my life would be very different now."

In any case, the intermittent relationship seemed now to have become the norm for them, and Weston did nothing to hide his interest in Xavier's sister, Elisa Guerrero, whom he was openly courting without concern for Modotti.

The successive nights spent partying were interrupted suddenly when Modotti received news that her mother was seriously ill. She left at once for San Francisco to be with her. For Modotti, returning to the United States was an abrupt verification of just how much her life had changed. Only a few years had passed, but nevertheless she felt no attachment to anything there. The lush oasis of San Francisco was for her a strange world compared to the boiling magma of Mexico City. While her mother's health improved, she tried to make the most of her stay in California by trying to sell her little old Korona so she could buy herself a large-format Graflex. In the letters she wrote Weston she asked him to understand her decision to part with the Korona, which had been a gift from him and therefore was tied to an era that was now coming to an end.

I feel so attached to it but you won't think me ungrateful for trying to sell it? I explained in my last letter the reason and I can't get one without selling the other. There is much I want to talk to you about—all my impressions of the U.S., all my reactions—all my ideas of working differently in photography when I return. . . . When it comes to doing things for myself, I just feel impotent—I don't know which way to start or turn—you know what they say about a prophet in one's own country. Well, in a way it works for me too—you see—this might be called my home town—well, of all the friends and acquaintances not one takes me seriously as a photographer—not one has asked me to show my work— only the ones I met through you. . . . I am going to work hard when I return to Mexico and differently—if I can get a Graflex—I have always been too restrained in my work as you well know but I feel now with a

Graflex I will be able to loosen up. This is all for now, dear, short but hardly sweet because I feel rather gloomy . . . but it is only temporary so—don't worry. . . .

In February 1926 Modotti returned to Mexico, determined to discover its other realities and to photograph its more unusual aspects. She traveled to the south with Weston several times, spending some time in Puebla and Oaxaca. They then headed back north, passing through Michoacán and taking the same road to Guadalajara that they had traveled previously by train, but this time they had no fixed itinerary. They journeyed through towns and villages whose faces and people took on a new dimension in Modotti's photos. She paid particular attention to the women, who often spoke to one another in ancient languages that had never been recorded, and who were remarkable for their simple gestures and the age-old dignity of their smiles.

On one of their stopovers they stayed in the capital and attended the opening of one of their exhibitions, which bore the subtitle "The Emperor of Photography and the Beautiful Tina Modotti: An Irresistible Combination." She had not had time to oversee the details of this exhibition, and she became furious when she read this. Once again her physical appearance was being emphasized over her talent as a photographer. Just as in Hollywood, her body attracted more attention than did her artistic expression. But this time the respected voice of Diego Rivera intervened. In the introduction he wrote:

Tina Modotti expresses a deep sensibility on a level that, still tending toward abstraction, unquestionably more ethereal and in a certain sense more intellectual, extracts the sap from the roots of her Italian temperament. However, her artistic work has flourished in Mexico, achieving a peculiar harmony with our very own passions.

Modotti's lifestyle inevitably changed as her new interests developed. Her house, which had been the center around which the most diverse people gravitated, became, little by little, just a stopping-off point between trips and excursions. Parties were less and less frequent, and the coming and going of friends tapered off. The renown of Modotti and Weston, a reference point of so many memorable nights, dissolved into the reality of daily life, where there was less time for the unconscious frenzy of living. Their paths were now diverging. Though the bond between Modotti and Guerrero was developing into a deep relationship, an affinity in which the intimate and the political were profoundly related, this is not what excluded Weston from Modotti's life. Although he continued to love her, he was not able to share his decisions with her, and he retreated even more into his skeptical individualism and hopelessness regarding the possibility of fighting for any kind of ideal. He also felt that he had come to the end of what for him had been a phase, and Mexico no longer conveyed to him the feeling that it once had. He began to miss his other children again, and Brett, who was becoming very fond of photography, wanted to return to California. Weston did not delude himself into thinking that he could convince Modotti to go with them: She might never find a solution for her restlessness. He was the only one who knew her well enough to understand that, but he also knew that there, in Mexico, she could continue searching for it.

In November 1926 Weston boarded a train headed north.

> The leaving of Mexico will be remembered for the leaving of Tina. The barrier between us was for the moment broken. Not till we were on the Paseo in a taxi rushing for the train did I allow myself to see her eyes. But when I did and saw what they had to say, I took her to me. . . . Tina with tear-filled eyes. This time, Mexico, it must be *adios* forever. And you, Tina? I feel it must be farewell forever too.

The big house on Veracruz Avenue was now empty. Tina stayed there a few days listening to the echoes, and she felt great pain because of Weston's absence. She did not regret the decision she had made, but she did not want to lose the contact that was still present in the atmosphere either, an understanding that could not disappear with distance.

> *Edward: I woke up with the nice feeling that you were here—My first thought was, I wonder if Edward is up yet? But the illusion did not last long—and the vision of your and Brett's empty rooms hurt me as much*

as yesterday after my return here—I want to write you at length, Ed-
ward—but not now—I cannot see now.

You know the poem of Ezra Pound on page 172.* You are that to me
Edward—No matter what others mean to me you are that—only you
were embittered and had lost faith in me—but I never did because I re-
spect the manifold possibilities of being found in all of us and also be-
cause I accept the tragic conflict between life which continually changes
and form which fixes it immutable.

Modotti moved to a tiny apartment in the center of the city on Abraham Gonzáles Street, a few minutes from the Zócalo, from those towers
that she had once been able to see on clear days from the terrace of her
house in Tacubaya. She converted a small room into a darkroom and
went back to working with perseverance, not worrying about her health,
having finally found the discipline she had always lacked. Her Graflex
became a merciless spy that saw the misery and suffering, captured the
desolation, but also exalted the anger of the organized protest. Workers'
hands holding their shovels, worn out by dust and sweat; puppeteers'
hands marked by veins swollen from fatigue; an Indian woman's hands
washing tattered clothes on a stone darkened by the sun. . . . For Modotti hands were the origin of the world. They created all things and
transmitted to material things the spirit that emanated from the heart.

People burst into her photos like a sea of hats converging at a demonstration, gathering around a copy of *El Machete* read by a farmer who
had been taught by the now-forgotten literacy campaigns. Somber, ener-
getic, passionate, disillusioned faces, scattered in the crowd of a demonstration, all looking to scrutinize a speaker standing on a platform.
Weak, exhausted bodies wandering about in rags that were too big due to
hunger. Bodies of children huddled on a street corner, the burned-out
look of a bad childhood. Poverty was a crime, and Modotti's photographs
screamed and affirmed this without false compassion. But there was al-

---

*Translator's note: *Modern American and British Poetry*, edited by Louis Untermeyer, has
Pound's Canto LXXXVI on p. 172, which begins: "What thou lovest well remains, / The rest is
dross. / What thou lov'st well shall not be reft from thee. / What thou lov'st well is thy true her-
itage. / Whose world, or mine or theirs, or is it of none?"

ways dignity in these images, a pride that history—the history written by the conquerors with the blood of the conquered—never managed to subdue in the Mexican people.

Her work began to break through geographical and political barriers. It was published by *Creative Art* in the United States, by the prestigious *Agfa Paper* in Prague, by *Variétés* in Brussels, and by the *British Journal of Photography*. Tina Modotti had opened the door to social documentary, the genre that would be immortalized by Robert Capa, David Seymour, and Gerda Taro. But for them photography would be their mission in life, while for Tina it would only be a means, a transition. And just when she had reached the most expressive stage in her photography, she would decide to leave it in the name of a revolution she would never see.

Part Two

INTO THE MAZE

Five

The Mexican Communist Party (Partida Comunista Mexicana, PCM) was founded in 1918, three years after the Chinese Communist Party. In 1923 Guerrero, Siqueiros, and Rivera became members of the Party's executive committee. At first art burst into politics with its aggressive creativity, shattering old patterns and imposing a feverish rhythm on changing values. But by 1924 the conflict between Trotsky and Stalin had already been resolved in favor of the latter, who in a few years would again acquire firm control over the "brother" parties. The "reason of state," that is to say, of the Comintern, had to prevail over revolutionary emotions. And certain behaviors in the Mexican cultural environment were regarded as dangerous "deviations" from the strict Soviet morals.

Guerrero was the most inclined of the three to accept Moscow's directives. Siqueiros was willing to fall into line; because he had fought with Carranza against Zapata's Ejercito del Sur, suppressing the rebels and siding with the strong man of the moment was a natural choice for him. He felt no conflict between the epic grandeur of his artistic work and obedience to the orders of his superiors. Deep down he had a military spirit: Respect for superiors was not to be discussed, and all "traitors" had to be eliminated without hesitation.

Rivera, on the other hand, was a restless spirit, attracted by excesses and unsuited to the Party's discipline. He was a true Communist in the most complete sense: In the immediacy of the reality he saw, felt, and seized, and not in the logic of the balances and subtle maneuvers that regulated the management of power. He was in constant search of something new, as much in the artistic as in the political arena. In 1927 he enthusiastically accepted the Soviet government's invitation to paint a mural on one of the buildings belonging to the Red Army. In Moscow, Anatoly Vasilyevich Lunacharsky extended the offer to him personally. When he arrived, he was named professor of the School of Fine Arts and began work at once on what was to be a large mural. But after only a few months, his ideas would differ totally from those of socialist realism. The guardians of Stalinist morals attacked his avant-garde art, which they considered too removed from the "receptive capacity of the people." And they especially had no tolerance for his extravagant and unpredictable behavior. In May 1928 Rivera left the Soviet Union, harboring a disillusion that would be the seed for what would happen a few years later.

But what would eventually truly separate him from his colleagues would be his deep roots in what could be defined in short as his "Mexicanness." Every one of his gestures responded to the instinct that bonded him to his land, where life manifested itself in violent contrasts and paradoxes, in the indecipherable harmony of apparent disorder, in the lack of discipline, natural generator of the creativity that was present in all Mexicans. Communism as Moscow understood it, and the line imposed by the Comintern on a country whose way of life was the complete opposite of Soviet strictness, led Rivera unconsciously to exaggerate everything that for him was the essence of Mexicanness.

Guerrero, unlike Rivera, gradually became a solid member of the Party. They named him the "statue of rock" for his somber silence and unchanging expression. He could not forgive Rivera for his need to dominate the stage and his need to be the center of attention: He nourished a pent-up resentment against him for having always been left in his shadows as an artist (overshadowed by Rivera's fame, Guerrero did not get the recognition he deserved for his participation in the Chapingo murals).

The resentment and political differences he felt inside would eventually turn into a stubborn hatred. He gave up painting and decided to devote all his time to militant politics. Modotti saw in him that security that she had always lacked—the invulnerability to doubts and indecision. Following Xavier's path meant anesthetizing the pain of a restless existence, renouncing a susceptibility that consumed and tormented her, and choosing instead an all-engrossing faith.

Modotti joined the Mexican Communist Party in 1927. Always in the first row at demonstrations and present at all activities as a tireless organizer, she spent much of her time working at *El Machete*, translating articles and foreign policy analyses. Having been conceived as an outlet for revolutionary artists and writers to express themselves, it had now become the official organ of the Party. Its founders were charged with using language for the avant-garde who were cut off from the masses, thereby alienating those who were accused of being "individualistic small bourgeois." With Guerrero, *El Machete* took on a tone and content that came directly from the Comintern.

For Modotti, photography continued to be a compromise and her only means of support. But it was an activity that had to be subordinated to her work as a militant, and she often had no time to stroll for hours in search of an image, much less travel around without a fixed itinerary or fixed dates. Her relationship with Guerrero was not easy to define. Their emotions could be read in each other's eyes and interpreted in the rare calm gestures that transmitted a natural and mysterious sensuality. Guerrero did not aspire to be understood. He did not explain how he thought and did not try to convince anybody of anything: To love him Modotti could only feel what he felt and respect his impenetrable character. She admired him for his strength and the determination with which he traveled his chosen path, and she accepted him without questions, without trying to change him. But the magnetic attraction she felt for his obsidianlike face, his sculptured body—and those eyes that scrutinized without surprise as if they had already seen everything that had ever been seen through the centuries—was not enough to turn a union of intentions into passion. Next to Guerrero, Modotti finally felt free of her reputation as a femme fatale, a view still held by many, which contributed to her acquiring a reputation that in some cases was somewhat dubious.

The poet Kenneth Rexroth, who in those years was spending a lot of time in Mexico City, did not know Tina personally, but he described her based on what he had heard:

> There was a café where they all hung out with heavily armed politicians, bullfighters, criminals, prostitutes, and burlesque girls. The most spectacular person of all was a photographer, artist's model, high-class courtesan, and Mata Hari for the Comintern, Tina Modotti.

With Guerrero she did not need to justify anything nor did she have to defend herself from all the foolish remarks being made about her. For Guerrero it was the essence of a person and not appearances that mattered.

When the Comintern called him to Moscow, Guerrero did not hesitate. Modotti did not object; she agreed that a militant had to put his duty before his feelings. But she was hurt that he did not express any sadness when he told her about the imminent separation. For Guerrero their relationship was not over, she would always be his, and the months or years they would be apart could not and should not change anything. If he did not return to Mexico, Modotti could join him one day in Moscow. For Guerrero the word "good-bye" meant nothing.

Six

In 1927 Modotti met a man who would change the course of her life profoundly and irreversibly: He arrived in the United States with an Italian deportation order for subversive activities in the name of Enea Sormenti, but in Mexico he went by the name of Carlos Contreras, a Spanish national. However, in files belonging to OVRA, the Italian fascist secret police, there was a thick dossier that identified him as Vittorio Vidali, from Trieste, an agent of the Bolshevik GPU.

Trieste was so close to Udine that when he spoke of it, Modotti seemed to inhale the atmosphere of her city. Their friendship was spontaneous and immediate. Vidali had an unusual character and conveyed sincere happiness; he loved wine but was willing to forego it at any time for tequila; he smoked more cigarettes than she did and lacked any moral attitude with respect to vice or virtue. Extroverted, somewhat prone to showing off, and loose with his language, Vidali confronted problems head on, totally convinced that blame, if any, could never be his. At first Modotti found him attractive for his friendliness and his graceful manner, but she at once noticed that within the Party people spoke about him cryptically and used strange winks and looks that revealed everything while specifying nothing. Among the leaders, Vidali had an aura of tacit respect, and he had a charisma that intrigued Modotti and increasingly aroused her curiosity. But she did not give in to the temptation to ask about his past or why the Mexican Communists regarded him differently from other newly arrived Party members. As usual, Modotti watched and listened without saying anything, absorbing what went on around her.

Her first encounter with Vidali had taken place in the middle of thousands of people and a sea of flags and posters that flooded the immense Zócalo. It was one of the countless demonstrations for Nicola Sacco and Bartolomeo Vanzetti, the two Italian anarchists condemned to die in the electric chair in the United States.

It was only a few days before the sentence was to be carried out, and, as the hours passed, the futility of the international movement became clear. Modotti found herself hunched over her papers, absorbed in translating into English a report on the stages of the trial and the inadmissibility of the evidence against Sacco and Vanzetti, whose conviction dated back to 1921. Vidali was the only one left at Party headquarters at that hour of the night. He went from one filing cabinet to another looking up entries and records, breathing heavily and muttering obscenities. Every so often she noticed his scrutinizing look, but she did not look up, and he continued to work noisily, as if he were bothered by the attention Modotti was paying to her work and not to him. When he went to look at some files that were scattered on the table next to her, she leaned back in her chair and let out a weary sigh.

"It's not true that you don't suffer," she suddenly mumbled, staring at the blackened ceiling.

Vidali stopped what he was doing. He looked at her out of the corner of his eye, waiting for her to explain.

"There have been many cases in which they have had to repeat the electrical charge. And even if it kills you the first time, it's not true that it lasts only one second."

Vidali rested a pile of papers on the table and turned to look at her with an interrogating smile, nodding his head and closing his eyes with an expression that she recognized.

"The electric chair," Tina persisted, in a monotone.

He nodded, then searched his pockets for his cigarettes, taking out a pack that contained only one. He shrugged and lit it. He took two deep drags and passed it to Tina, saying, "You are always thinking about happy things."

"I don't think that all these demonstrations and peaceful protests are doing any good; they're going to kill them anyway."

Vidali let out a strange little laugh, as if he liked the hint of rage he detected in her voice.

"Perhaps they're of no use in sparing them from execution. . . . But those two unlucky ones are not what matter most. Thanks to them, millions of people around the world have finally seen the real face of the United States government. So those demonstrations have been good for something."

She watched him, shaking her head slightly. Then, as she passed the cigarette back to him, she looked straight into his eyes and said, "For me the idea of two innocent people writhing in an electric chair is more important than anything else."

Vidali nodded, and, as he took his last, long drag, he raised his other hand as if to calm her. "Of course, of course . . . don't misunderstand me. But when you say 'two innocent people' I don't think that is the question; that is to say, I don't care at all if they committed the robbery and all the rest or not, because I'm convinced that taking money from someone who has it in order to finance an organization is sacred. That is not my idea of innocence and culpability."

"Take it easy," she interrupted. "It's not mine either."

"I know. That's why I'm talking about it with you and not with the others. But let's get one thing straight: Someone is guilty, very guilty, when he lets himself be caught, bringing disaster to dozens of people and years of work. Period."

Modotti, her arms crossed, held his gaze. There was an unusual expression on her lips, the hint of a smile of defiance.

"You never have doubts, do you?"

Vidali took a few steps with his hands in his pockets, casting an indecipherable look her way. He stopped and, suddenly serious, said, "Doubts are a luxury that we still can't afford. Every one of our hesitations is like a door left open. And *they* are always ready to go in. Because those who are on the other side of the wall, Tina, have very few doubts, believe me."

She stared into the darkness of the large room for a few moments. Then, impulsively, she began to organize her papers with a sudden burst of energy that drew her out of her tangled thoughts.

"Maybe you're right," she murmured, "but the only thing I'm sure of is that I envy you."

Vidali laughed, and his voice resounded in the silence, startling Tina, who nevertheless did not stop opening and closing drawers and filing folders and papers.

"What do I have that you envy?"

"The certainty that you're never wrong," she responded without looking at him.

"When someone is convinced that he is doing what he should, no mistake can take away the certainty in what he is doing."

Modotti turned the key in the last drawer and put it underneath a book that was behind her. She turned and looked at Vidali's face, illuminated by a single lightbulb hanging from the ceiling.

"It's hard to explain. You know . . . I am also convinced that I am doing the only thing that can be done right now. And everything else . . . has become less important than it was before. Only that . . . I can't manage to talk about two *compañeros* who are about to be electrocuted simply as a means for getting people together, for sensitizing a public opinion that may be completely forgotten by tomorrow!"

"Calm down, calm down. We're mixing up a lot of things here that need to be separated and evaluated one by one," Vidali said, grabbing her by the arms.

Modotti was impassive, but she was aware of the heat of his hands that were holding her, and they alone explained more than words what it meant, for the man in front of her, to have the invulnerable certainty of acting appropriately. They were determined hands, hands without even the slightest tremor. She felt the impulse to take them in her own and look at them so she could study every line and vein in order to try to understand his past and to read the present.

"Tina, sometimes the distance that we need to keep with respect to certain events is confused with cynicism. But that doesn't mean that every one of us does not feel what you say you are feeling. And you have to understand that our power lies precisely in this, in suppressing certain emotions. Because if we didn't do so, we would let ourselves be carried away by impulsive reactions that would, without a doubt, lead to our defeat."

Now his hands stopped squeezing her so tightly, and his fingers moved over her arms slowly, like a soothing caress that conveyed an unknown sense of calm.

"The feeling of defeat, Tina, carries with it a poison that takes root little by little and eats away at you, leaving you unable to fight. If you allow it to work its way in, if you don't drive it back with your will, any later attempt to resist it will be futile."

He moved away from her, putting his hands back in his pockets. Then, looking out of the corner of his eye, he added, "And maybe we should also begin to give more importance to certain words. *Compañeros*, for me, is a word that has a very specific meaning. And I don't use it very often. . . . Look, Sacco and Vanzetti are symbols, and they have to be defended for what they represent. But they are anarchists, and as such I do not consider them to be my *compañeros*. The fact that today they are fighting against a common enemy does not mean that they cannot, one day, become enemies. What puts us on their side right now is just a battle, a skirmish—but in order to gain power a larger war is necessary, and maybe none of us will see the end of it."

Modotti stared at him with a look that faded into sadness. She shook her head as if she were going to refute something, but then turned around and went to get her shawl that was hanging from a hook on the wall, leaving suspended the answer she was unable to give.

Vidali looked over a file and, distracted, observed Modotti's silent movements, her body that glided through the light and shadows of the dusty room full of piled-up newspapers, mismatched furniture, flags, and rolled-up posters.

"Wait," Vidali suddenly said when he saw her drop the office keys on the table. "It's very late . . . I should go with you."

She looked surprised.

"I thought you had to finish that work—"

"I'll come right back. Anyway, your house is nearby."

She nodded with a half smile and a look as if she were giving up, and then added, "Don't be so sure that Mexico City is full of barbarians like they told you up north."

Vidali pulled on his felt hat, put on his jacket, removed his ever-present revolver from the drawer where he had stored it and placed it in the holster at his waist. He smiled openly and happily, offering her his arm with theatrical gallantry, and said, "If that is so, you, too, are different from how they described you."

Modotti stopped in the doorway and looked at him closely, but he avoided her eyes.

"May I ask what you're talking about?" she asked him, trying to joke with him.

"Drop it. It was supposed to be a compliment, but in the end it never comes out right."

They left, taking Mesones Street in the direction of Lázaro Cárdenas Avenue. Vidali looked at her strangely and whispered, "Anyway, one of these days I will try to express myself better."

Seven

Modotti's relationship with Weston was now limited to their intense letter writing, although as the months passed her letters became more infrequent. Weston had decisively chosen a world that, although not opposite to hers, was different and had nothing in common with hers. And yet he continued to be the only one to whom she could communicate her anxieties and conflicting feelings, those internal voices that she forced herself to suppress as she spent day and night putting all her energy into her work with International Red Aid, the close network of trade among the anti-imperialist associations in Latin America, and even into the founding of an antifascist committee of Italian emigrants in Mexico. She was able to let herself be swept up by an enthusiasm that Weston would never feel, such as when she described to him her visit to an experimental school for workers' children, and children from the streets, which was run according to democratic and antiauthoritarian methods. She did not try to convince him, nor did she try to explain to him the appropriateness of her decisions. She avoided set phrases, easy slogans, and the words that were repeated in proclamations and meetings, and she did so effortlessly, because it was a language with which she would never be able to identify.

Photography continued to be the thread that connected them. They exchanged photographs and shared the impressions and feelings awakened by these images. When she received a series of photos from a study that Weston was doing on the spirals of shells, Modotti's reaction showed the instinctive and uncontrollable excitability that he, and only he, knew so well:

> *My God, Edward, your last photographs surely took my breath away. I feel speechless in front of them. . . . I just cannot look at them a long while without feeling exceedingly perturbed—they disturb me not only mentally, but physically—there is something so pure and at the same time so perverse about them—they contain both the innocence of natural things and the morbidity of a sophisticated, distorted mind. They make me think of lilies and of embryos at the same time—they are mystical and erotic.*

Modotti had no regrets, and she was convinced that the path she had chosen merited all kinds of sacrifices, but she did not want Weston to think that he no longer mattered to her or that she had gotten over him, because her new life did not discount the passionate time they had shared.

> *You don't know how often the thought comes to me of all I owe to you for having been* the one important being, *at a certain time of my life, and when I did not know which way to turn, the one and only vital guidance and influence that initiated me in this work that is not only a means of livelihood but a work that I have come to love with real passion and that offers such possibilities of expression (even though lately I am not making full use of these possibilities).*

Although photography did not provide her with a life of comfort or economic security, it did give her what she needed to live. She earned the minimum amount she required in order to spend the greatest amount of time possible in political activities, activities that would very soon attract the attention of Italian spies.

On May 12, 1928 in *El Machete*, Modotti signed a petition to participate in a demonstration in memory of Gastone Sozzi, a young worker who
had been murdered in a jail in Perugia, where he had been imprisoned for
antifascist activities. An OVRA agent who was working for the Italian
Embassy had infiltrated the crowd of demonstrators with the goal of identifying the signatory and making a report. On July 3, the Ministry of Foreign Affairs sent the following telegram to the Ministry of the Interior:

> The Royal Legation in Mexico informs us that on May 11 a poster ap-
> peared on the walls around the capital with the headline "Against Fascist
> Terror," the work of the local Communist Party, which called its people
> to headquarters to protest the supposed murder of Italian worker Gas-
> tone Sozzi. This demonstration was not deemed newsworthy, since there
> is an insignificant number of Communists, barely surpassing one hun-
> dred, in the Mexican capital. Therefore it would not have been worth
> mentioning had there not been among those addressing the group two
> Italians, whose names were unknown among our compatriots until today.
> Their names are probably false, or they arrived recently and therefore we
> have no information on them. Both have said they represent the Anti-
> Fascist League, and they have used extremely violent language against
> the Regime. One of them is a man called Enea Sormenti, who claimed
> to be a fugitive from Italy and seemed to preside over the meeting. The
> other person is a woman called Tina Modotti, who has described the Italy
> of today as "a large prison and a vast cemetery."

The Ministry of Foreign Affairs immediately decided to open a "Tina
Modotti dossier" and discovered a notation on a Modotti dating back to
February 1926, in which the Italian Consulate General in San Francisco
denounced Tina's brother Benvenuto as an "active anti-Fascist" belonging to a subversive group called "Vindication."

It was the beginning of constant surveillance of Tina by OVRA, which
would also treat her family mercilessly in their attempt to lead her into a
trap set by their agents, whose goal was to repatriate her and prosecute
her. Part of the family correspondence was intercepted and, when OVRA
was not able to achieve its main objective, fascist counterespionage
would follow some of Modotti's distant relatives. Dino Modotti, Tina's

cousin, emigrated to Bolivia in 1926, where he worked at all kinds of jobs, including that of traveling photographer. In Bolivia he thought that he would finally be able to express the anarchist ideas, repressed for so long in Italy. But he did not know that because of his last name OVRA was constantly on his trail, until 1933, when the Italian Embassy was able to get the Bolivian Ministry of War to arrest him. After being forced to write a letter of renunciation, expressing total support of the fascist government, he was released. But he was a marked man, and amid misery and persecutions he would decide to end his life at the age of fifty, firing a bullet into his mouth.

Modotti, who knew nothing of this, did not hide her commitment as a militant, a commitment that grew more and more blatant, unlike that of Vidali, who gradually distanced himself from public acts and carefully avoided being noticed outside meetings. In order to earn a living, but also so she could send a small sum to her mother every month, Modotti increased her workload, mostly taking photos commissioned by *Mexican Folkways*. She also took a job photographing Orozco's murals. One of the three best Mexican muralists, José Clemente Orozco, too, regarded artistic and revolutionary activity as inseparable. But his anarchist tendencies set him further and further apart from Siqueiros and even Rivera. He felt that Communism the way they understood it in the Party had nothing to do with him because it did not form part of his land and his people.

When Xavier Guerrero moved to Moscow, Modotti's apartment was transformed once and for all into a workshop. It was so filled with negatives, acids, and prints that there was scarcely room left for visitors or the old evening meetings with friends. But Modotti never refused hospitality to foreign militants who were passing through; and so the address on Abraham Gonzáles quickly came to be better known than that of Party headquarters. She spent the remainder of her time working at *El Machete*, quickly becoming indispensable to the editor, Rosendo Gómez Lorenzo.

One afternoon in June 1928, Julio Antonio Mella entered the small office, which was always full of correspondents. Modotti had already seen him at some demonstrations, but this was the first time that the young Cuban noticed her and showed a special interest in her. Gómez Lorenzo introduced them, suggesting they go for coffee together.

Leaving the office, the editor smiled to himself: The two did nothing to hide their mutual attraction. Later Mella accompanied Modotti home, covering the short distance to Abraham Gonzáles in a heated discussion about Modotti's photography, which he had admired for some time, and about Cuba, to which he swore he would return at once to foment the revolt against the dictatorship.

Eight

J ulio Antonio Mella was still in school when the din of the October Revolution reached Cuba, immediately finding fertile ground there among those oppressed by a colonialism that, over the centuries, had changed faces and mottoes but not methods or goals. Mella was impressed by Lenin and fervently pored over the few writings that he had managed to obtain, and then traveled to nearby countries in search of more of his books. But he was also fascinated with that commander of the Red Army who had guided his men into battle in an armored train replete with cannons and machine guns: Lev Davidovich Bronstein, better known as Trotsky, who moved tirelessly from one end of the immense steppe to the other, attacking the White anti-Soviet divisions of Generals Anton Denikin and Pyott Wrangel without letup.

In 1919 Mella moved for a few months to Mexico, where he began to write a book that would be titled *Diario de viaje* (Travel Diary). In this work his feelings for places and people were combined with political considerations and a criticism of the pillaging perpetrated in Latin America by old and new colonialism. When he returned to Havana he enrolled in the School of Arts, where he quickly made a name for himself as the leader of the university protest movement. Endowed with great communications skills, he influenced the many rebellions and theorized on collective and individual direct action; he was also the mastermind behind the unification of the university struggles with those of workers and farmers. He founded and ran the magazine *Juventud* and became the leader of an anticolonialist study center that would become the Universidad Popular José Martí. In 1923 General Machado unleashed a wave of repression that would result in Mella's expulsion from the university for sedition. In 1925 he, along with Carlos Baliño, organized the constituent congress of the Cuban Communist Party, but shortly afterward he was arrested because of a bomb explosion in the Payret Theater, an event that the government used to weaken the opposition, accusing the Communists of the attack. Mella refused any legal defense and at once began a hunger strike, which in eighteen days triggered a vast mobilization around the island. Party leaders did not approve, as they considered a hunger strike to be an individual form of struggle and believed that only bourgeois intellectuals, who had enough food, could allow themselves not to eat as a sign of protest.

The demonstrations multiplied, and the government chose to neutralize the explosive potential by releasing him. After being freed, Mella decided to evade a second arrest by going into exile, where he would be able to continue his activity against the dictator. He went ashore in Honduras and crossed into Guatemala, from which he would enter Mexico in 1926, obtaining political asylum from the government of Plutarco Elías Calles. Named to the executive committee of the Anti-Imperialist League of the Americas, he traveled to Brussels in February 1927 to represent the League at the World Congress against colonial oppression, and then to Moscow to attend the International Congress of the Syndical Organization.

When he returned to Mexico he directed all his energy toward the creation of the Confederación Sindical Unitaria Mexicana, formed to oppose the powerful yellow syndicate of the Confederación Regional Obrera Mexicana (CROM). But he did not renounce the main objective of his political commitment: to organize an expedition to Cuba and instigate the insurrection.

.   .   .

Mella was tall and athletic, with a face that expressed the passionate energy with which he confronted life and a penetrating gaze that could in-
stantly display a childlike tenderness. He had an impulsive, impetuous
character that ran counter to the Byzantinisms and underground maneu-
verings of the Party apparatus, and was unaware of the cynicism of its
officials. His way of speaking and his gestures reflected a sensuality, a
carnality that came from the nature of the Caribbean island, made up of
violent contrasts and an innate gentleness. Modotti fell deeply in love
with Mella and she realized that she had never felt such intense emotions; he loved her with frenetic, urgent passion, with the same tireless
rhythm with which he had lived every minute of his twenty-seven years.
He called her Tinísima and wrote her short, passionate love letters when
he could not see her for even just one day; he burst into her life like a
tropical hurricane. In September 1928 they decided to live together, and
Mella moved his typewriter and his books into the already chaotic fifth-
floor apartment. He had to leave immediately for Oaxaca because of political commitments, and from there he wrote to her:

> *I haven't forgotten your face once on this whole long journey. I still see
> you "in mourning"—clothing and spirit—saying your last good-bye as if
> you wanted to come toward me.*

Modotti continued to be regarded by all as "Xavier Guerrero's woman,"
and within the Party there was no lack of critics faulting her for having
fallen in love with Mella when Guerrero had just left. Mella could not
imagine the internal anguish that Modotti was living with; she ques-
tioned not only the loyalty she felt she owed Guerrero but her colleagues'
lack of understanding as well. Guerrero's sister, Elisa, did not miss the
chance to state publicly that Tina had never loved her brother, and that
she had deceived him all along. A few days later, on September 15, 1928,
Modotti decided to clarify once and for all her relationship with Guerrero, and she sent a long letter to him in Moscow.

> *There is no doubt that this will be the most difficult, most painful, and
> most terrible letter I have ever written in my whole life. I've waited a long*

time before writing it, mainly because I wanted to be very sure of the things I am going to tell you and secondly, because I know from the start the terrible effect that this will have on you. I need all the calm and serenity of spirit I have to explain to you clearly, without ambiguities; and above all, to keep myself from getting emotional, which would be inevitable if I let myself think of what this letter represents for you. . . .

But I should tell you what it is I have to tell you; I love another man. I love him and he loves me, and this love has made it possible for something to happen which I thought could never happen; to stop loving you.

Guerrero chose to remain silent. There was no response to Modotti's letter which, nevertheless, seemed to have freed her, at least in part, from a crushing weight. Although she felt some remorse for ending her relationship with Guerrero, at least she had been honest. And Mella, with his overwhelming presence, left her no time to worry about it.

Modotti did not tire of photographing Mella, and in dozens of photos the many facets of his personality shine through in his face. For those who did not know him well there seemed to be a world of difference between his profile, with his determined look and tensed muscles, and the same face caught by surprise when asleep, his eyes closed and his wavy dark hair spread out on the pillow. Only when he slept, with a natural smile on his face, did Julio become a twenty-seven-year-old young man, free from the premonitions of death that hung over him more and more each day, despite his refusal to accept them.

Together with Modotti he managed the Hands Off Nicaragua Committee, the organization supporting Augusto César Sandino's fight against U.S. occupation. He continued writing for *El Machete*, working nonstop on the small typewriter immortalized by Modotti in a photograph that anticipated a certain modernist aesthetic.

He also founded a new magazine he called *Tren Blindado* (armored train). The choice of name was not accidental, and in Moscow, some would interpret it as a confirmation of its Trotskyite tendencies—a provocation that could signify an irreversible conviction. The decisive confrontation between Trotsky and Stalin had taken place in 1924. The idea of the "permanent revolution," defended from the start as a necessary means to defeat Western imperialism, was in opposition to the "revolution in a single country" advocated by Josif Vissarionovich Dzhugashvili, otherwise known as Stalin, the man of steel. After Lenin's death, the ambitious Georgian wove a subtle and complex web of alliances within the Party that undermined Trotsky's personal and political power. The enormous charisma Trotsky had throughout the Soviet Union did him little good. In January 1925 he was forced to leave the Commissariat of War; in October 1926 he was thrown out of the Politburo; and in the summer of 1927 he was expelled from the Central Committee. Three months later Stalin had him thrown out of the Party. Trotsky had no choice but to go into exile.

The hard and ruthless fight between the two opposing concepts of socialist revolution extended to all the so-called brother parties. And in Mexico this conflict would become one of the bloodiest.

The Comintern considered the PCM to be the basis for Muscovite ideology on the American continent. The actions of the victorious line in Mexico City were destined to influence all future Latin American struggles. Stalin relied on a Central Committee made up of extremely loyal leaders, close to whom nevertheless emerged charismatic figures who were dangerously drawn to Trotskyite ideas. Vittorio Vidali was sent to Mexico to support precisely these loyal leaders. His task was to force the opposition to declare itself openly, following the *operative* orders that would arise.

Julio Antonio Mella never openly sided with Trotsky, but given his firm commitment to fomenting insurrection in Cuba, there was no possibility of his agreeing with Moscow. Every guerrilla center represented a danger to the Comintern's consolidation of power in the Soviet Union because its existence could provoke attacks from the capitalist powers. During this time Communist parties had to work almost exclusively to prevent armed uprisings in their respective spheres of influence.

At the Fourth International Congress of the Syndical Organization (Congreso de la Sindical International), Mella met Spanish Communist Andrés Nin, who explained to him the theory of "Leftist Opposition" on the politics of collaboration among the classes defended by Stalin and Nikolay Bukharin. Argentine leader Victorio Codovilla immediately circulated an internal document that demanded Nin's expulsion for deviationism, whereby a meeting was held in which his proposal would be put to the vote. Mella shared Nin's opinions, but he was aware that he could not allow himself to express them openly, which would isolate him. Still, he did not want to become an accomplice in Nin's expulsion either, so he decided not to be present for the vote, sparking an immediate reaction from Codovilla, who applied pressure on all agencies under his influence to organize a smear campaign against the Cuban. When the congress proposed to elect a delegate to represent Latin America on the leadership of the International Communist Party, the majority supported Mella's candidacy. But Codovilla, backed by the Right, wove an intricate web of accusations against Mella that would lead to the desired result: the election of the Venezuelan Ricardo Martínez, a man with ties to Codovilla and a staunch adversary of Mella.

When Mella returned to Mexico, he set aside his differences and tried not to get involved in the internal fighting, intensifying organizational efforts and promoting demonstrations and debates against the Sixth Pan-American Conference, which was laying the foundation for a new imperialist hegemony in the Western Hemisphere. But he did not accept the Comintern's imposed condition of abandoning insurrectional objectives, and with his friend Sandalio Junco, he established the National Association of New Emigrants in Cuba, whose aim was to prepare an armed expedition in 1929. As a result of this, tension increased with the PCM leaders, whose relations with the Cuban Communists were already on the verge of a confrontation.

At the time Mella arrived in Mexico, the Party was facing a serious internal crisis due to the gulf between the reality of the country and the directives from Moscow. Between the second congress in 1925 and the fourth congress in 1926, a split had developed between the leadership of Guerrero, Siqueiros, and Rafael Carrillo, and the right wing of Galván, Edgar Woog (known as Stirner), and Díaz Ramírez, which advocated an alliance with some sectors of the government. This sectarianism was leading the Party down a blind alley, and the turn toward the right for the International imposed by Bukharin in 1926 would rock its foundation. A few days later, the PCM substantially modified its political line and lent its support to the "nationalist, revolutonary" government of Elías Calles. Mella bowed to the conditions of the Comintern, but he would later create new opposition with respect to syndicate elections.

Álvaro Obregón was elected president for the second time, succeeding Elías Calles. As general of Carranza, he had participated in the bloody suppression of the rebellion of Zapatistas and Villistas, and his missing arm could, in fact, be blamed on Pancho Villa, who had himself cut it off during the battle. In 1923, and now as president, Álvaro Obregón found that the occasion to seek revenge would coincide with the interests of the United States: Twelve hired assassins laid an ambush for Villa in the little town of Parral, riddling his car with bullets. Conservatives called Obregón "the Mexican Lenin," but he preferred to sum up his philosophy of government in a phrase that would later become the emblem of a political class: "There is no such thing as a general who can stand up to a fifty-thousand-peso gunshot."

In 1927 Mella launched an offensive against the syndicates of CROM, and the division in the Communist Party paralyzed any initiative by the opposition. He maintained that the moment had arrived to exploit the circumstances and form a new central syndicate of leftists. However, CROM was so corrupt that the large worker base ran the risk of becoming divided in the face of governmental attacks, and without waiting for the Party's decisions, the Cuban set to work reorganizing the syndicate struggle. At the fifth PCM congress in April 1928, Mella and his group presented a proposal supporting the imminent dissolution of CROM and the current crisis of the anarchist Confederación General de Trabajadores (CGT), but they were in the minority and were defeated by the leadership, which saw in the initiative a subsequent division of worker power. Mella did not yield to the Party's decisions and, together with other militants, he continued the work he had already begun. The Central Committee then accused him of attacking its unity.

A few days later a syndicate conference was held in Montevideo, Uruguay, at which Codovilla and Martínez asked for Mella's expulsion from the Party for insubordination. The Central Committee settled on a compromise: Mella would have to condemn Trotskyism publicly and renounce the ideas of the Left opposition; in return he would be named national secretary. All this occurred on the eve of the Sixth International Congress in Moscow.

On July 17, a Catholic militant shot President Álvaro Obregón dead in a restaurant. Immediately afterward it came out that CROM leaders were responsible for the crime. The Communists had to reconsider the posture they had maintained until then, and Mella, the rebel who continued to reject the logic of the Party machine, went back on the attack. Taking advantage of the disintegration that had resulted from gross errors committed by the leadership of the Right, he silenced the conservative Stirner and, with Diego Rivera, decided to go up against the intransigence of the Comintern in Moscow and even Stalin himself. Supported by representatives of the workers and farmers, he won the vote that was held on the new central syndicate. The leaders of the International were forced to denounce the blow, and they allowed the organization of the Confederación Sindical Unitaria Mexicana. Stalin did not respond, reacting with only a faint smile that his adversaries would quickly learn to recognize: the slow approval of a good-natured father, which foreshadowed imminent revenge. It was his way of expressing absolute condemnation, and he would wait years in some cases, and only months in others, for this revenge.

In September 1928 Stirner asked for the expulsion of Julio Antonio Mella for "the crime of working against the party line in the leadership of syndical dualism." He was supported by Xavier Guerrero, Rafael Carrillo, and Vittorio Vidali. Many centrist leaders had rightist inclinations, forming a front against the Left headed by Mella and Rivera. They had waited for the Moscow delegation to return in order to launch their offensive again. The conflict paralyzed the project, which nevertheless had been approved by the International, and Vidali proposed a syndicate made up exclusively of Communists, provoking the withdrawal of the CGT anarchists from the organizing committee and the abstention of many syndicates that had split from CROM. The Party ran the risk of splitting up permanently, and Mella was summarily removed from the Central Committee and isolated. Under the absolute prohibition of organizing an expedition to Cuba, he stopped collaborating with the Party. It was December 1928, one month before his murder.

During a heated meeting at Party headquarters on Mesones Street, Vittorio Vidali lost control and approached Julio Mella, shouting in his face, "Don't you ever forget that there are only two ways to leave the International—thrown out, or dead."

Nine

The stems appeared first, standing out against the gray background, imprinted by the moods of who knew how many hands. Then the chiaroscuro isolated the whiteness of the two flowers, a winding pair of calla lilies that reached toward the light, toward the highest point, divergent and separated by a subtle boundary of empty space that prevented their contact. It was a photograph Modotti had taken almost a year earlier, which she had now decided to reprint in one of the many magazines that enabled her to survive.

Calle. Modotti said that Italian word in her mind and wondered what relation it could have with the Spanish word, identical yet with such a different meaning. In Mexico that flower was called *alcatraz.* For an instant she saw San Francisco again, the faces and the years that now belonged to another era and another world—*Alcatraz.* Who could have been so cynical and so cruel as to name a prison in San Francisco after such a sensual flower? A flower that, with its graceful form, looked like a symbol of recovered freedom, the emblem of a carnal nature, throbbing with the heat of the sun, an invitation to shower it with cool rain, a call to fertilize it with life.

The water broke down the remaining acid, the image materialized on the paper, and the two calla lilies rose to the surface as if wanting to break through the dimension to which they were confined. Modotti picked up the photo with the tongs, shook the paper as she held it up high, and hung it from the cord stretched across the center of the small room.

She drew open the black curtain and saw Mella's back bent over the typewriter. He was motionless, hunched over the keys. He turned around, smiled faintly, and stared off into space again.

Modotti took a few steps toward him and reached out her hands to stroke his hair. But she stopped quickly, frozen by that glassy stare that penetrated her like a ghost.

"Julio—"

He moved slightly, surprised, as if hearing his name troubled him. Then he nodded his head and sighed, approving the silent question he read on her face. He got up, smiled again, and hugged her violently, desperately.

She buried her face in his chest, and he breathed in the smell of her soft hair.

"You should always wear it like this, Tina," he whispered, his fingers touching the back of her neck, caressing it slowly.

She looked up, searching his eyes, which remained fixed on her hair.

"Don't pull it back again," Mella said in a voice hoarse with sadness, in a tone of sorrow that she noticed with a sharp pain in her soul.

He moved away and went back to the table. He looked for his cigarettes, crumpled up the empty pack, walked around the room a bit, and stopped next to the window. The sky was violent, with a reddish clarity that burned from behind the thick cumulus clouds. The sun was about to disappear. The air was dry, suddenly cold from the absence of the sun. The rainy season was far off.

"Who knows where I will be when the rain returns," he murmured, staring at the high clouds that glided by.

"You'll be here, with me," Modotti said, in a tone that revealed both reproach and request.

Mella turned around abruptly.

"With you, yes, maybe. But not here."

She threw herself into his arms. She shook her head and, her eyes filling with tears, said, "I'm begging you, Julio, you are alone. All your *compañeros* are against you. You have to understand."

"*Compañeros?*" he hissed, his eyes inflamed with anger. "My *compañeros* are in Cuba. Here . . . there is only a handful of power hungry bureaucrats. Hybrids without hearts or feelings. . . . For them, our land is just a province a little farther away than Siberia. . . . They are renouncing their blood, do you understand?"

"Julio, you don't want to see—"

He took her face between his hands, which were trembling and did not know if they should hug her or push her away.

"Tina, listen to me. . . . You are not like them! You can't get mixed up with those . . ."

His voice died out in his throat. He leaned over and kissed her on the lips, barely touching her. Then he turned to look out the window again. She hugged him from behind, resting her cheek against his back.

"Do you remember those photographs of yours . . ." he said softly. "The ones of the puppeteer's hands. . . . That is what they are turning into. Hanging from threads, blind and deaf, convinced that there is only one reality and one leader. Ideals, feelings, passions—everything has to be destroyed in the name of the Party. This is not what we wanted—this is not why we have sacrificed everything."

He took her hand, which rested on his chest, and kissed her palm. Then he moved away from her, put on his jacket, and said, quickly and coldly, "I'm going to the magazine. I have to look at an article again."

She moved toward him, rushing to kiss him, with a frenzy that did nothing to hide the fear in her eyes.

"I'm begging you, Julio. Let time take care of things. This is a terrible time, you can't keep confronting situations like this."

Mella smiled, threw his head back, and opened his arms. For a minute he had become again the boy from years past. But now happiness was an effort that never diminished the deep line on his forehead.

"Don't be afraid, Tinísima. What do your Mexican friends say? 'There is more time than life. . . .'"

He headed toward the door and left without looking back. Modotti heard the echo of his footsteps on the stairs, the pounding on the steps taken in threes, and the muffled sound of the front door, which hung for a few seconds in the motionless air of the small apartment.

The blood seeped through the light-colored sheet they had thrown over him. A dark red stain soaked the yellowish cloth, glistened for a second, and immediately dulled again as it passed under the lights in the endless corridor. A trickle of blood ran down the arm that hung down from the stretcher, leaving a trail of dark drops on the gray stone floor. Modotti broke away from the police, who continued to ask her a repetitious litany of questions, and ran after the group of nurses, reaching him and grasping the hand that hung lifeless. It was cold, icy like the partially rusted metal of the gurney. But in a few seconds life flowed back into his fingers, intertwined with hers, squeezing them with his last bit of energy.

Mella opened his eyes and looked desperately for Modotti's face. She leaned forward, still running behind the gurney. The noise of shoes in the corridor and the squeaking of the rusted wheels created a bloodcurdling racket, the obscene roar of death that kept watch on his eyes, still alive. When they stopped to open the door to the operating room, he finally saw her: He raised his head, trembling from the effort, whispered something that only she could hear, and softly caressed her cheek with the palm of his bloody hand. He smiled faintly, closed his eyes, nodding with great difficulty, and squeezed the arm with which she cradled his head one last time.

"Don't leave me, Julio, . . . don't give up," Tina whispered, swallowing her tears.

He let out a painful sigh that was interrupted by spasms caused by the blood filling his lungs. He drew her to him, and before they could move him through the door he managed to say, *"Now there is no time . . . or life. . . ."*

He disappeared into the blinding clarity that illuminated a steel table surrounded by white figures and fragments of inexpressive faces. The image lasted a second before the doors closed suddenly.

An oppressive silence exaggerated the moans of others who were dying around her. Dismal echoes, indistinguishable voices of others' suffering, confusing noises. Quick, strong footsteps of a man coming closer, running. Modotti realized there was someone behind her when the panting became the only distinguishable sound.

It was Sandalio Junco, eyes wide with distress and anger in a dark face that glistened with sweat in the shadows. A look that wanted to accuse her, but that in a few seconds was clouded by an overwhelming sadness. He opened his mouth and his voice died away, because now there were no longer any words that made sense. He stared at her in silence, shaking his head to contain the pain that he was not able to release in one liberating scream.

Modotti looked down, squeezed her temples between her hands, and seemed to grow smaller in that body of hers, which was suddenly bent and lifeless.

Sandalio fell back, hit the wall, and came to rest with his hands behind him on the icy tiles. He inhaled the sickly sweet air of decomposition and disinfectants until he was dazed. Then, with stony calm, he moved away from the wall and looked, for the last time, at that motionless figure of a woman in the middle of the corridor.

"It's over—now everything is really over," he said in a small voice, exhausted. He walked slowly toward the exit, slipping by a group of policemen and journalists who had burst in with a deafening clamor.

Mella's death marked the point of no return for Modotti. Now militancy became the only refuge that could protect her from her doubts and distress. *The Party is always right* was the anesthetic that enabled her to overcome her uneasiness, the answer to all her uncertainties. One month after the murder, a ceremony commemorating Mella was held at the Hidalgo Theater, during which she stated, "They have murdered not just the enemy of the Cuban dictatorship, but the enemy of all dictatorships. We maintain that it was General Machado who gave the order."

But when she wrote to Weston, the torment of her uncertainty regained the upper hand, and denying the past in order to keep herself from looking back was a painful decision for her.

Oh, Edward, for a few moments to be near you—to be able to give vent to all the pent-up emotions which gnaw at my heart—you might not agree with all I would say—that does not matter—but you would understand the tragedy of my soul and feel with me—and that, not everybody can do!

But I cannot afford the luxury of even my sorrows today—I well know this is no time for tears; the most is expected from us and we must not slacken—not stop halfway—the rest is impossible—neither our consciences nor the memory of the dead victims would allow us that—I am living in a different world, Edward—strange how this very city and country can seem so utterly different to me than it seemed years ago! At times I wonder if I have really changed so much myself or if it is just a kind of superstructure laid over me. Of course I have changed my convictions, of that there is no doubt in the least, but in regards to mode of living, tastes, new habits, etc.—are they just a result of living in a certain environment, or have they really taken the place of the old life? I did not make this very clear; I mean: are these new habits taken up in order to keep pace with the new environment, or have they really taken the place of the old life? I have never stopped to question this before and I cannot understand why I am doing it now.

Someone decided to help her calm her internal anguish, someone who was by her side to support her with all the strength of his absolute convictions. Vittorio Vidali—with his unyielding faith tied to the myth of action—possessed a special energy, an extraordinary seductive ability. In the days following Mella's murder he disappeared into thin air. Security reasons, he would later explain, and in fact his role and activities in the Comintern justified such precautions. He did not explain himself, but he always found time to be with Modotti, to spend long hours in heated discussions, and personally to make sure that her silent torment did not develop into a dangerous crisis.

Part Three

PHOTOGRAPHY
AND MILITANCY

Ten

Modotti had met Frida Kahlo the previous year, at the time when José Vasconcelos was attempting to prevent Pascual Ortiz Rubio's rise to power as Obregón's successor. Vasconcelos's campaign was unsuccessful in defeating Rubio, one of Mexico's most corrupt and authoritarian presidents, but at any rate, the opposition had contributed to consolidating the wave of awareness that had spread to the student masses and would, a few months later, achieve political autonomy for universities. Kahlo had approached the Communist Party, and in Modotti she found a likeness and an immediate friend.

Kahlo's life was marked by pain. In 1925, two months after her eighteenth birthday, she boarded a bus that crashed into a train en route to Xochimilco, a suburb located a few kilometers from the city. Frida had remained conscious among the twisted metal plates. However, she was motionless, looking at the first rescuers to arrive on the scene almost with surprise, more amazed than frightened. Only when they attempted to get her out did she let out a scream so piercing that it paralyzed the arms reaching out for her: An iron bar had penetrated her back, passing all the way through her.

Doctors had given up all hope for recovery, and when her desperate and stubborn desire to cling to life thwarted the already planned funeral, everyone thought she would be confined to a wheelchair for the rest of her days. Clenching her teeth every night so as not to scream, Kahlo forced herself to survive in a cast that tortured her constantly; she resorted to morphine when the pain threatened to drive her mad. Month after month, soaking her bed with tears and sweat, biting the pillow to hold back the groans, Kahlo regained strength, leaving the doctors who had been taking turns studying this unique case perplexed. Two fractured vertebrae, eleven fractures in her right foot, a dislocated left elbow, a perforated abdomen, acute peritonitis—and, nevertheless, exactly ninety days after her brush with death, Kahlo left her house in Coyoacán and walked, with the support of crutches and squeezed by the cast, to the bus that would take her downtown.

She had taken it upon herself not only to face the Zócalo filled with people, but also to endure the horror that rose in her throat each time the bus stopped or turned abruptly. Her miraculous recovery, however, would be followed by even greater suffering, with relapses that would make it unbearable for her to look at herself in the mirror. But as time went by, Kahlo formed a permanent relationship with her pain, from which she drew the vitality for artistic creation. She was a painter of dreams, her surrealism saturated with that Mexicanness that made fun of death with a macabre irony. She painted self-portraits in which her face, with its enigmatic smile, overshadowed her broken body. In her work, split between oppressive reality and liberating symbolism, the beauty of her own nakedness affirmed its supremacy over the torture of a plaster cast and a prosthesis for her crippled leg.

She had in common with Modotti her perception of an erring past more than her renunciation of a militant present. Kahlo was eleven years younger, and her participation in the Communist community was not a sacrifice but rather a need for her to rebel. Modotti was drawn by the strength she observed in Kahlo, by the determination with which she took back her life. Kahlo began to frequent the house on Abraham Gonzáles Street, attended dinners and discussions, and amused herself by provoking the moralism of the austere officials by wearing bright-colored dresses and displaying a natural sensuality. With Kahlo nothing was the result of a momentary affectation; her actions did not respond to a need to call attention to herself, but rather to her independent instinct, which ran counter to anything conventional.

One night in the summer of 1929, Kahlo was at Modotti's house, where a group of friends had gathered to have a little tequila as they talked and listened to music. The atmosphere was very different from the feverish vivacity that used to make the house on Veracruz Avenue vibrate with shouts and laughter. The sporadic conversations seemed to show the effects of the humid heat that had invaded the city after a brief storm. The rainy season had begun, but in the valley of Mexico City a sultry atmosphere of gray, sticky air had hung over the city for days. It was evening when the massive figure of Diego Rivera entered the room. Everyone turned toward the newly arrived guest, certain that his love of being the center of attention would give a sudden spark to the general lethargy of the evening.

Rivera let out a impatient sigh and wiped his sweat on the sleeve of his crumpled jacket, covered with varnish stain. He glanced over at the bulky phonograph that was playing the whining notes of an old song. The antiquated mechanism was skipping revolutions, dragging the sounds with annoying squeaks. Rivera grimaced with displeasure. He unbuttoned the only button that fastened his jacket over his fat belly and pulled a gun from his waistband.

A deafening shot rang out, leaving everyone dumbfounded and paralyzed. The record spun around a few more times before stopping with a final squeak of the broken machinery.

Rivera smiled and looked around him, as if he had just saved them all from a slow suicide. Dramatically he blew into the barrel of the gun and put it back in his pants, with some difficulty. Nodding her head resignedly, Modotti muttered, "And now he expects them to applaud him," and she went to sit next to Kahlo. Unlike the others, Kahlo could not stifle her laughter.

"Don't worry," Rivera said, turning to Modotti as he poured what was left of a bottle of mescal into a beer bottle, "I'll give you the new one I just bought on the black market in Tepito. And I'll also bring you decent records that may help change those funereal faces you're all wearing."

He took a sip of mescal, smacked his lips, satisfied, and looked around for an empty chair. When his eyes met Kahlo's, he made a curious gesture and began to study her without the slightest shame. He approached her slowly, and she cocked her head to one side, continuing to look straight at him, not at all embarrassed.

"Tina," Rivera said, without looking away, "now that we have inevitably met in your home, would you be so kind as to introduce us?"

"You don't need anyone to introduce you," Tina replied. "Your entrance is unmistakable."

"We've already met," Kahlo interceded, extending her hand. Rivera kissed it and held it a good while as he frowned, searching his memory for that delicate face with such dark eyes and thick eyebrows.

"I used to be a student at a school where you were painting a mural," Frida added.

After a few seconds, Diego opened his eyes wide and made a strange grimace, as if an old grudge had suddenly popped back into his head.

"Ah, yes—that unbearable little girl who made me lose time."

He patted his belly and exclaimed, "I told you to go to the devil because you were always getting in my way, and you—you took to soaping up the corridor so that I would break my neck!"

"I did worse things," Kahlo said, laughing, and her eyes sparkled. "I was the one who hid behind a column and started to shout that your wife, Lupe, was coming, while you were busy studying *anatomy* with one of your models."

Rivera nodded reproachfully and feigned an expression of satisfaction at this unexpected bravado.

"You see, I liked this much less," he said, finally letting go of her hand to go look for a chair. Then he sat down next to Kahlo, leaning toward her, and whispered, "Tell me something, only light in this house of shadows: Was I blind or were you still inside the cocoon waiting to become a butterfly?"

"Let's just say that . . . *you* were too busy with your work."

Diego sighed regretfully.

"Work, work, and nevertheless I have yet to begin the most beautiful of my paintings."

He took her hand again gently.

"Do you want to pose for me?"

On August 23, 1929, the newspaper *La Prensa* announced the marriage that had taken place two days prior between *maestro* Diego María de la Concepción Nepomuceno Estanislao de la Rivera y Barrientos Acosta y Rodríguez, and the painter Magdalena Carmen Frida Kahlo, de Rivera. At first Kahlo's parents were not at all in favor of the relationship. For them Rivera's fame as an artist was completely secondary to his being a womanizer and a drinker. Moreover, he was a Communist.

And as for "appearances," Rivera, in addition to having been born in 1886, twenty years before Kahlo, was very ugly, gigantic, and clumsy. When seen together they were described as "the elephant and the dove." But when it came to conquering the hearts of those to whom his fame and his revolver initially meant nothing, he possessed unsuspected gifts of kindness and geniality. And in less than two months, Kahlo's parents were convinced that there could not be a more affectionate and sensitive man to whom they could entrust their daughter. A few days before the wedding, her father spoke to Rivera aloud and said, "Well, Diego, the time has come to warn you: Frida is a charming and intelligent girl, but she has a demon inside her. Do you understand? A hidden demon."

"I know," Rivera responded with a look of naive innocence.

"So much the better, then. I've done my part."

This remarkable union that, contrary to predictions, would last the remaining twenty-seven years of Frida's life, did not have any influence on their respective artistic paths. Diego's painting was directed outward, motivated by great social changes, and it was monumental in proportion; Frida's was intimate, sensitive to small details, and capable of capturing the immense strength of subjective passions.

They shared their disappointments and the painful decision to isolate themselves because of their common political ideals. After Mella's death, Rivera felt that the Party, of which he was one of the leaders, was betraying the revolutionary essence that had given it life. Communism, for Rivera, was above all the affirmation of human and social values whose goal was independence—not only from a political and economic point of view, but a cultural one as well, understood as respect for the demands and ways of life in each country. After the authoritarian and centralizing turn taken in Moscow, a break was now inevitable.

In any event, Rivera and Kahlo tried to avoid a direct confrontation with Modotti, knowing that she was a tacit supporter of the new direction. The day after Mella's murder, Rivera had defended her, sincerely believing that she was in the middle of a police setup aimed either at deflecting the investigation of Machado or at hiding the Mexican government's responsibility as planner and executor of the crime. But as the months passed his doubts grew, and keeping quiet, with only his blind faith in the Party, became increasingly difficult.

A few weeks after the wedding, Rivera and Kahlo organized a dinner at Modotti's house, and for a few hours that joyful desire to be together that had united them all in previous years was recreated. Music, conversation, bottles of tequila, cases of beer, wild dancing in the small open space—Rivera picked up the delicate Kahlo and knocked over furniture, spinning around wildly.

At some point Rivera's ex-wife, Lupe Marín, arrived. She was friends with everyone there, and her attitude quickly dispelled any worries: She toasted the couple, laughed out loud, and joked honestly with Kahlo, warning her about what awaited her.

But a short time later, the tequila tore off the mask of understanding altruism that Marín had been wearing. Going over to Kahlo with an open smile and the appearance of wanting to praise the young beauty, she shouted, "Friends, may I have your attention for a moment! Look carefully at what I am about to show you."

And when all eyes were on her, she suddenly lifted up Kahlo's skirt and then her own.

"This is what Diego has been reduced to. Now he prefers two wooden sticks to all that I have given him."

She departed abruptly, leaving a silence behind her.

The party had been effectively ruined, despite everyone's effort to recapture the climate of euphoria, pouring drinks and laughing. Kahlo withdrew to the terrace to swallow her anger and make an effort to stay, so that the weight of the situation did not fall on Modotti. Rivera, meanwhile, drank until he lost control, and nobody managed to take his gun from him in time. Completely drunk, he began to shoot at the ceiling while the few who remained threw themselves behind chairs and sofas. He smashed a terracotta vase into pieces, hitting it right in the middle. He cursed and shouted that they were all a bunch of cowards and traitors, and that they referred to each other as *compañeros* but that they would have their own children hanged in exchange for a little power.

Modotti stood in front of him and stopped him, taking hold of his wrist with both hands. And she whispered softly, "You, Diego, will do more harm with your tongue than with your damned gun."

Kahlo walked across the room, picked up her shawl and headed for the door. Rivera decided to follow her, bent over, his face filled with sadness.

Before he left, he turned to look straight at Modotti. He said, "I'm drunk . . . and maybe I'm crazy too. But what I said . . . is the truth. And you . . . you know it better than I. You chose to be silent, and I can understand that. But you can't expect me to do the same."

In October 1929, Diego Rivera was expelled from the Party. The alleged reasons were only pretexts, his having agreed to paint murals for the "counterrevolutionary government," for example, and giving in to "individualist and small bourgeois ambitions." In fact, Rivera had already openly adhered to the "Left opposition" and did not hide his sympathies for Trotsky. Modotti, only eight months after the painter's defense of her freedom and her reputation, did nothing to oppose Vidali's accusations and those of other leaders loyal to him. With icy detachment she wrote to Weston:

> *I think his going out of the party will do more harm to him than to the party. He will be considered a traitor. I need not add that I shall look upon him as one too and from now on all my contact with him will be limited to our photographic transactions. Therefore, I will appreciate it if you approach him directly concerning his work.*

Modotti ended her friendship with Kahlo this way too, eliminating her from her life in the name of her beliefs. They would never see each other again.

Eleven

In spite of everything, 1929 was Modotti's most active year as a photographer. On December 3 an exhibition dedicated solely to her work opened at the National Library, the first after many group shows in which Weston's work had been the main artistic attraction. To mark the occasion, Siqueiros gave a lecture entitled "The First Exhibition of Revolutionary Photography in Mexico," in which he stated, "An art form that reflects and retains what it sees, and offers us, thanks to the purity of its expression, the surprise of being able to record what until now the observer could only see."

Modotti wrote an introduction to the catalog that could be regarded as her "manifesto" on the new conception of photography as a means to interpret reality, in contrast to all those who wanted it to be seen as a purely aesthetic search.

> I consider myself a photographer, nothing more. . . . Photography, precisely, because it can only be produced in the present and because it is based on what exists objectively before the camera, takes its place as the

most satisfactory medium for registering objective life in all its aspects, and from this comes its documental value. If to this is added sensibility and understanding and, above all, a clear orientation as to the place it should have in the field of historical development, I believe that the result is something worthy of a place in social production, to which we should all contribute.

Inaugurated by the rector of the Universidad Nacional Autónoma de México, the exhibition was widely covered in the newspapers and was a noteworthy public success. The same newspapers that had portrayed Tina as an ambiguous figure with indecent habits were now praising her work and her great artistic sensibility.

A young critic, Gustavo Ortiz Hernán, who would later become the editor of *El Universal Gráfico,* wrote an article full of praise in which, among other things, he maintained:

Without a doubt, Tina Modotti's photographs are profoundly original and differ from any other production. Ideologically Modotti belongs to the avant-garde and to the more extreme tendencies of the social movement in which she is one of the most significant members. Her works can be classified with relative ease: pure composition, in which concern for perspective, construction and dimension reveal the artist's skill in using her own instrument. Floral compositions, vases, tools—all form a unique genre of still life manipulated with great plastic sense. There are two photos, above all, that should simply be titled "Revolution," a perfect synthesis of a social ideology: in the first one, you see the neck of a guitar, an ear of corn and a cartridge belt; in the second one, a sickle is in the place of the guitar.

An especially beautiful photograph, on the other hand, falls into another category: the composition of crystal glasses in which the aesthetic characteristics blend harmoniously with a rhythm and a musicality felt by association of ideas. The suggestive power of this image is huge. The perfect synchronicity of the transparencies is magnificent.

Scenes of daily life appear in another group: photos of construction sites, stairs, stadiums, telegraph wires. . . . Everything we are used to seeing every day and to which we are normally indifferent acquires consistency and personality, even an esoteric nuance. Tina Modotti's photographs symbolize the aspirations and anxieties of the new generation about knowing everything, the need to examine and delve into things, to discover all aspects of reality.

One of her photographs, destined to be perhaps her most famous, is that of Julio Antonio Mella's typewriter. Sentence fragments are visible in the upper right-hand corner of the paper inserted in the carriage, calling to mind her essay on artistic inspiration. Modotti had the same quote printed on the poster announcing her exhibition. But when she had to send a copy to *Mexican Folkways* for publication, she would carefully erase the wording.

What Mella was writing when she took the photo was no more than a fragment taken from one of Trotsky's books, on the relationship between art and modern technology.

Twelve

The Hands Off Nicaragua Committee proved to be Modotti's greatest political commitment that year. Despite the Comintern's efforts to stifle any insurrectional tendencies, the U.S. invasion of the small Central American country aroused the independent spirit of the entire hemisphere. In addition, Sandino benefited from special support in Mexico, where he had lived in 1921, working as a skilled laborer in the petroleum-producing installations of Cerro Azul, Veracruz, which belonged to the American-owned company Huasteca Petroleum.

Nicaragua's troubled history was characterized by incessant civil wars and invasions, during which even a psychotic adventurer like William Walker, who had come from Tennessee to head an army of U.S. mercenaries paid by the Vanderbilt financial group, was able to proclaim himself president in 1855. In 1912 the United States military occupation began, with the landing of the first marine contingents. The country was an important strategic point, where plans to build an interocean canal preceded those in Panama. The plans in fact called for widening an already existing route, formed by the San Juan River, which joined the Atlantic with Lake Nicaragua, from which the Pacific was easily reached. English and Dutch pirates themselves had already conquered the river, bombarding the Spaniards in Grenada, located on the opposite shore. Three million dollars were paid for the rights of concession, considered as national debt that would justify the formation of a control commission that would become the country's true administration. When Panama was later chosen for the site of the canal, Washington could not afford to have any other powers one day decide to build a second canal, and the destiny of Nicaragua endured the practical application of the Monroe Doctrine. When the U.S. "backyard" showed destabilizing tendencies, the marines intervened to restore order. In 1914 Mexico experienced the effects as they landed in Veracruz, which sparked the vigorous resistance of the entire population of the port city.

In 1926 Sandino regrouped the original nucleus of soldiers, who were immediately defined as "the Army of Madmen": Their undertaking was in effect considered madness by the U.S. high command. With sixty men they sought to resist forces not only greatly superior in number, but also better armed and equipped. But in just a short time Sandino proved to be a strategist not to be underestimated. Unable to confront the enemy in open country, he chose the harsh mountainous region of Las Segovias as a base for his guerrilla attacks. (Centuries before, this region had been a refuge for the Indians resisting Spanish rule.) He chose red and black for their flag, in memory of the syndicate struggles in Mexico, where it was an established custom to display red and black outside occupied factories. And once he had eight hundred guerrillas under his command, he began to carry out a series of attacks that would threaten for years the five thousand marines from the U.S. contingents. Statements from the *Indio de Niquinohomo* began to circulate secretly throughout Nicaragua.

I am Nicaraguan, and I am proud to have Indian-American blood running through my veins, the blood that contains the atavistic mystery of a loyal instinct for independence and rebelliousness. I am a plebeian, as the oligarchs and the clucking hens who are always willing to bow their heads say. It is an honor to be born in to the bosom of the oppressed, who are the spirit and the backbone of this race. The greats of history will say that I am too small for this undertaking. But my insignificance has the advantage of a heart that does not tremble, and with our swords we swear to defend the national dignity and to redeem the oppressed. Our ideals embrace the wide horizon of internationalism and the right to be free and to demand justice, even if it means spilling our own blood and the blood of others.

And you, herd of morphine addicts who trample on all rights for your own benefit, come. Come murder us on our land. But know that we are waiting for you steadfastly, and we don't care how many heads or guns you have. Know that one day the destruction you are sowing will fall on your greatness and will shake the foundations of the Capitol and turn the white cupola of your famous White House, the sordid den where you plot crimes and genocides, red with blood.

On July 12, 1927, Capt. G. D. Hatfield, commander of the expeditionary force marshaled in Ocotal, sent an ultimatum to Sandino, who responded immediately: "We will never surrender. We are waiting for you. Here nobody is afraid of you. *Patria libre o morir.*"

Four days later the Battle of Ocotal broke out: twenty hours of ruthless, often hand-to-hand combat, during which even air power, bombing towns and encampments, was used in an effort to try to make the rebels fall back. Sandino did not liberate Ocotal, but news of his resistance against forces ten times greater than his own spread throughout Central America.

The warship *Raleigh;* the destroyers *McFarland, Preston,* and *Putnam Pauling;* and the transport ship *Oglala,* replete with marines and field cannon, set sail for Nicaragua on January 4, 1928. But, as the Sandinista guerrilla motto says, "The mountains do not betray anyone." The U.S. troops, which fought using tactics and procedures from World War I, suffered grave losses in every battle. Despite the intense use of artillery and air power, which devastated towns, causing civilian deaths for the first time in history, the guerrillas continued attacking hard, thanks to their thorough knowledge of the terrain and the tactics of rapid disengagement. It was the support of the people that proved decisive. Farmers supplied them with food, offered shelter to the injured, and built entire platoons of straw figures to trick the bombers while the columns advanced or fell back to the opposite slope of a mountain. And they suffered fierce retaliation after every ambush as the U.S. troops struck back for their inability to defeat the Army of Madmen.

Their shortage of ammunition and medicine was the Sandinistas' weak point. Most of their weapons came from conquered depots or were collected after they won a battle. The long years of war made it necessary to initiate frequent contact with solidarity movements in neighboring countries, among which Mexico had an extremely important role. Germán List Arzubide was a member of the Hands Off Nicaragua Committee, despite the fact that his relationship with the Communist leadership was not as close as in the past. The Estridentista poet organized meetings and demonstrations to raise funds, with which he purchased medicine that two Venezuelan exiles, Gustavo Machado and Salvador de la Plaza, delivered to the Nicaraguan guerrillas. As a sign of gratitude Sandino presented the committee with a U.S. flag that had been captured in combat and asked that they take it to the anti-imperialist congress that was about to begin in Germany. List Arzubide, who for lack of money could not travel directly from Mexico to Europe, went to the United States, trying to sneak aboard in a port farther north. To cross the border, he wrapped himself in the flag, concealing it beneath his clothes. He arrived in Frankfurt the day before the congress opened, and he managed to get to the congress just as deliberations were beginning. With the bullet-riddled Stars and Stripes bearing the words *Nicaragua libre* on his shoulders, List Arzubide crossed the immense room as everyone stood up to sing "The Internationale."

In 1929 Sandino decided to travel to Mexico City to obtain political and economic support. He was accompanied by Agustín Farabundo Martí, the ideologist of the Salvadoran insurgent movement, who had moved for a time to Nicaragua and had become one of his lieutenants.

The previous year Julio Antonio Mella had been one of the most avid supporters of the Nicaraguan cause, and his death marked a progressive deterioration in relations between the Mexican Communist Party and Sandino. Given the situation, Sandino could not afford to acknowledge subtle distinctions between Party line, bourgeois deviationism, or ideologically reactionary forces; the support offered him by the Mexican government, although minimal, had to be regarded as a point of strength against Washington's expansionist politics. And the petitions from the Communist leadership to break such a relationship were obviously rejected by Sandino, and their statement of denunciation was similarly ig-nored. It would have been suicidal for him to renounce one of the few al-lies he had on the South American continent.

In fact, the Comintern had decided to boycott the Nicaraguan strug-gle, using every means. Stalin wanted to gain Washington's sympathies in order to keep the United States as far away as possible from the con-flict, which now had to be sustained by European powers, and "back-yard" politics could become a tacit agreement on the respective spheres of influence. Sandino, moreover, had very little in common with Bolshe-vik ideology. In his encampments "The Internationale" was sung, and his writings advocated the establishment of a socialist society. But San-dinismo was an amalgam of direct action and deeply antiauthoritarian thought, based on a respect for individual differences and on the indispu-table affirmation of national sovereignty. Although the self-determination of nations was a sacred and unrelinquishable point for Sandino, he was nevertheless prepared to accept the abstentionist impositions of Mexico and the rigid Party structure.

In Mexico, where he had lived from July 1929 until February 1930, he received some demonstrations of popular solidarity but a cold recep-tion on the part of the Communist leaders, who were constrained by their sectarianism.

"We are troubled by this silence, the isolation, the despair at being so ignored. We must show the world that we are still fighting . . . the strug-gle in Nicaragua continues with the same intensity and fervor as before, but U.S. money has built a wall of silence around us," Sandino wrote in his diary.

While he was in the capital, a strange event took place: Tina Modotti offered to join the guerrillas. She wanted to leave Mexico and fight in the mountains of Nicaragua.

"And what did he say when you asked him?"

Vidali's voice shook Modotti from her thoughts. She stubbed out her cigarette in the ashtray full of butts, looked up, and stared at him for a few seconds. Then she shrugged and said indifferently, "Nothing. He just smiled."

Vidali continued walking around the room.

"Don't underestimate him. That Indian seems to have the ability to sense things by simply sniffing the air."

Modotti got up from her chair and went over to him, interrupting his nervous pacing between the door and the window.

"Vittorio, I thought I had made myself clear from the beginning. If I go there, it will be because I feel that I am suffocating here, and don't expect anything else from me."

He crossed his arms and studied her out of the corner of his eye.

"Then let me explain something to you. That caricature who goes around showing off with his sombrero and bandolier is doing exactly what Washington wants. Thanks to him they will reinforce their presence in Central America, and no matter how many he kills, in the end they will buy him just as they have done with all the 'great liberators' who preceded him."

"You always have an answer for everything," Modotti responded, turning to the other side.

"And you are losing your head. What the devil is the point of going down there to fire a few gunshots for a lost cause or, even worse, of being under the command of an adventurer who is showing clearly that his interests are contrary to yours? As soon as they offer him a post in the government, he will become one of the many puppets that can be moved as they want. And furthermore, the Party has already taken its measures. Sandino is a danger; it doesn't matter if he is aware of it or not."

"I don't like it, Vittorio. . . . I don't like your knack for solving problems. That is also why I want to go. Everything is changing too quickly, and I have the feeling that only by getting away for a while will I be able to see things with some clarity."

"It's all right," Vidali said, suddenly pleasant. "Go to Nicaragua. That is not the problem. Besides, we already have *compañeros* working in his ranks."

"Working?" she responded, looking at him with her eyes reduced to two slits.

"Yes, Tina. Working. They are building something immensely larger and longer-lasting than the little blond girls of some revolutionaries in novels and certain *caudillos* who wave the flag of nationalism in order to secure a seat in the government. Our project is so complex and delicate that we will not allow any demagogue to get in our way. Not one."

Modotti fell back into an old armchair. She closed her eyes and nodded.

"You don't have to explain it to me. You don't need to convince me."

"I know, Tina. I know that very well. In fact, I still trust you as I do few others."

"So what should I do, then?"

Vidali smiled and looked surprised, as if the answer were too obvious.

"Join the other *compañeros* and work with them, that's all."

"Right," she said, with a tired expression, "which means observing, taking notes, not taking risks—and sending a detailed report from time to time."

"It's not that simple. We need to know in time what is happening in dangerous situations in order to prepare for the actions of whoever wants to destroy us. Or at least in order to prevent injuries."

Modotti looked at him coldly, murmuring, "More or less what you do every time you go to Cuba."

Vidali remained motionless, holding her gaze without the slightest reaction.

"We got to Cuba in time," he said softly, "but there is still much to do. And we will do it. Until the end."

A few days later Modotti ran into Sandino at a meeting of the Solidarity Committee. The impenetrable face of the Nicaraguan Indian was veiled in sadness; the aid he had hoped to receive had been reduced to many promises, a few pesos, some boxes of ammunition and medicine, and a few old guns kept by former Zapatistas. As for Modotti's offer, he had decided that he could not accept it. Survival in the mountains of Matagalpa and Jinotega, in the forests of Chontales, in the marshes of the Atlantic coast was arduous, even for the toughest guerrillas who had been with him from the beginning. Modotti would not be able to do much for their struggle. Fighters were not what Nicaragua needed. What it needed was the help of those who, using the world "revolution" to open and close every vote, now turned their backs on those who did not want to wait any longer.

The silence cleared the way for a campaign to discredit Sandino. Stalin, who had already realized that he would never submit to the decisions of the Comintern, ordered a violent operation to be organized against him to be carried out by the Mexican Communist Party. In June 1930 *El Machete,* which now bore the subtitle "Central Organ of the Communist Party of Mexico, section of the Communist International," dedicated the first page to the "Betrayal of Augusto C. Sandino":

> The Nicaraguan guerrilla, allying himself with the counterrevolutionary government in Mexico, has become a tool of Yankee imperialism. If the anti-imperialist struggle is not closely linked to the world revolutionary movement, it becomes a small bourgeois struggle that looks for power only in Nicaragua. . . . On the Latin American continent it has no raison d'être if it is not supported by the respective Communist parties.

In a climactic crescendo of lies and insults, the newspaper for which Diego Rivera and Julio Antonio Mella had written defined Sandino as a "lackey of imperialism" and "renegade of Las Segovias." But, in spite of the isolation and the boycott, the Indian from Niquinohomo continued to defeat the invading troops and reject compromises with the régimes imposed by Washington. The most painful thing for him was the split with Farabundo Martí, who decided to remain connected to the Communist movement, even though Moscow would do everything possible to render him powerless. The day of his final good-bye, Sandino wrote, "We have said farewell with our hearts full of sadness, but with the harmony of our immortal friendship. Like two brothers who love each other but cannot understand each other."

On March 8, 1934, Sandino fell into the ambush set by the National Guard of Anastasio Somoza García. The feigned withdrawal of the occupation troops led him to enter into negotiations in order to put an end to the bloody civil war. But it was only a trap to murder him. The remarks in *El Machete* sounded like a sinister warning to all guerrilla leaders who dared to defy Moscow's directives:

> Sandino had betrayed the cause of the anti-imperialist struggle—the same one in which he had so brilliantly distinguished himself in the early

years—but all he had achieved has been to die like a poor devil. This proves, more than any theoretical explanation, the powerlessness of the small bourgeois *caudillos,* incapable of carrying the fight against imperialism to the end, a fight that only the Communist International consistently leads throughout the entire colonial and capitalist world.

The only voice that rose in Sandino's defense was that of Farabundo Martí, who grief-stricken, wrote the eulogy of a man who chose solitude rather than have to bow his head to anyone.

Thirteen

Sunday, February 5, 1930, was a typical sunny winter day in Mexico. In the capital, the inauguration was being held for Pascual Ortiz Rubio, whom the opposition had already derisively rechristened "Flor de té." After the ceremony the president left the National Palace with his family to go for a walk through the immense Chapultepec Park. His air of an enlightened monarch, who kindly greeted passersby and publicly seemed to be an affectionate father and faithful husband, did not seem to take into account the acute tensions that were tearing the country apart. The electoral campaign had been an increasingly intense series of confrontations and shootings, and numerous opponents had been summarily eliminated by the police or by unknown defenders of the established order.

A young man suddenly sprang out from behind a tree, pulled out a revolver, and shot Ortiz Rubio six times. Distance and the attacker's poor marksmanship saved the president. Only one bullet grazed him, slightly injuring his mouth.

A perfect opportunity: The press campaign against the red refugees who threatened civil coexistence in the country finally found a solid pretext. The plot could only have been set in motion by foreign agitators. And little did it matter that the would-be assassin, twenty-three-year-old Daniel Flores, was arrested and that no proof of his apparent connection to leftist elements was found. Repressive activity had begun, and in addition to thousands of arrests, deportation orders were handed out right and left.

Modotti was accused of having taken part in the planning of the attack and of being one of the "brains behind the operation." Imprisoned, she protested the only way she could: with a hunger strike. Thirteen days later she was notified of her deportation from Mexico and given forty-eight hours to leave the country.

The only friend to defy police control was the photographer Manuel Álvarez Bravo, who went to her house to see her while she packed the few things she would take with her. Half a dozen agents waited impatiently to accompany her to the station, where she would board a train for Veracruz and from there sail to the United States. Nervously she threw everything that did not fit in the few suitcases she had into the middle of the room, including most of her photos. Álvarez Bravo bent down to pick some of them up and timidly asked if he could keep them. Distracted, Modotti assented, forcing a smile for the bashful man who watched her with a pained and tremulous look of helplessness. Thanks to him, a few unpublished photos were saved, although the negatives would eventually be lost.

Álvarez Bravo hurried to the station, barely arriving in time to say his final good-bye. Apart from him and the police, there was no one else beneath the sign for the train bound for the port of Veracruz.

The *Edam* was not a passenger ship but rather a Dutch merchant ship, and Modotti embarked as a prisoner because her efforts to obtain a visa for the United States had been futile. Ambassador Dwight Morrow recognized her right to citizenship as the widow of Roubaix de l'Abrie Richey, but because she had no U.S. passport, he put the condition on the visa that she must make a written declaration in which she agreed to renounce Communist ideology and to cease to participate in political activities. When Modotti refused, the ambassador ordered Mexican authorities to prohibit her from disembarking at any port of call, forcing her to proceed to Rotterdam.

Despite the special security measures, Vittorio Vidali boarded the *Edam* at the port of Tampico, presenting a Peruvian passport in the name of Jacobo Hurwitz Zender. He was assigned a cabin and was completely free to move about. For the Mexican police he was a fugitive, keeping in mind the arrest warrant issued for Carlos J. Contreras. And among the infinite variety of ways he could have left Mexico, he chose precisely the ship that carried the deported Tina Modotti. The second port of call was in Cuba. Vidali went ashore and spent the two-day stopover on the island inspecting the operations of the Cuban Communist Party in his capacity as a Comintern official.

Modotti, on the other hand, was constantly watched and kept locked up in her small cabin while the ship was in port. On February 25 she wrote a long letter to Weston:

> I suppose by now you know all that has happened to me, that I have been in jail thirteen days and then expelled. And now I am on my way to Europe and to a new life, at least a different life from Mexico. No doubt you also know the pretext used by the government in order to arrest me. Nothing less than "my participation in the last attempt to kill the newly elected president." I am sure that no matter how hard you try, you will not be able to picture me as a "terrorist," as "the chief of a secret society of bomb throwers," and what not. . . . But if I put myself in the position of the government, I realize how clever they have been; they knew that had they tried to expel me at any other time, the protests would have been very strong, so they waited for the moment when, psychologically speaking, the public opinion was so upset with the shooting that they were ready to believe anything they read or were told. According to the vile yellow press, all kinds of proofs, documents, arms and what not were found in my house; in other words, everything was ready to shoot Ortiz Rubio and unfortunately I did not calculate very well and the other guy got ahead of me. This is the story which the Mexican public has swallowed with their morning coffee, so can you blame their sighs of relief in knowing that the fierce and bloody Tina Modotti has at last left forever the Mexican shores?

Dear Edward, in all these tribulations of this last month, I often thought of that phrase of Nietzsche which you quoted to me once. "What doesn't kill me, strengthens me," and that is how I feel about myself these days."

Two weeks later the *Edam* docked in New Orleans. Modotti's reputation as a dangerous subversive preceded her, and the city police did not trust the ship's security. Therefore Tina was locked up in a small room in the port police station.

I don't even remember when I wrote to you last, so much has happened in these past weeks and such unexpected things too—as for instance my presence here—but—have gotten to the point where I just accept philosophically what comes along. You know the old saying: "It never rains unless it pours"; well that just about fits my condition at present. I thought that after thirteen days in jail in Mexico City—followed by two days (all I was granted to get my things ready), and after being taken to Vera Cruz and put on a boat, via Europe, my troubles would be over— but no indeed—in the first place I learned that the boat [will take] one month and a half for a voyage that could be done in three weeks—but since on this boat passengers are accidental and its specialty is cargo, we stop at all the following ports: Veracruz, Tampico, New Orleans, Havana, Vigo, Coruña, Boulogne-sur-Mer, and at last Rotterdam. This would not be so bad if I traveled as a normal passenger, but in my condition of being expelled by the Mexican government, I am strictly watched in all ports and not allowed to touch ashore, excluding this port where the U.S. Immigration authorities brought me here, and here I am relegated for eight days, that is till the damned boat gets through its loading and unloading.

Journalists and photographers rushed to see and immortalize the "revolutionary of impressive beauty," as the headlines of the New Orleans papers would read the day after her arrival.

The newspapers have followed me, and at times precede me, with wolf-like greediness—here in the U.S. everything is seen from the "beauty" angle—a daily here spoke of my trip and referred to me as "a woman of striking beauty"—other reporters to whom I refused an interview tried to convince me by saying they would just speak of "how pretty I was"—to which I answered that I could not possibly see what "prettiness had to do with the revolutionary movement nor with the expulsion of Communists—evidently women here are measured by a motion-picture standard.

From every port Modotti sent Weston letters in which the progressive intensification of her political convictions was evident. She strongly resisted the temptation to give in to the pain caused by the continual uprooting and displayed the conviction of being able to work as a revolutionary in whatever country she was in. There was never the slightest remark about Vidali's being on board.

Modotti was thirty-four years old, had lost all contact with the photographic world, and had no means to support herself. She found herself alone once again and, once again, militancy was the only refuge she had left. Relying on the support of the Communist International was now essential. The price would be the rejection of any doubts or uncertainties, any distinction between comrades who erred and traitors.

Her interminable journey did not end when she arrived in Holland. OVRA had instructed the Italian Embassy to present an immediate order for her extradition. When the *Edam* arrived in Rotterdam, her record in the *Bolletino delle ricerche—Supplemento dei sovversivi*, (Research Bulletin—supplement of Subversives) signed by the chief of police in Udine, bore the order "Communist to be arrested." And according to a note sent by the Mexican Consulate, Modotti had asked to be issued an Italian passport several months before her deportation. The document, registered as number 3300, had been delivered on January 7. It is likely, therefore, that the measures taken by the Mexican authorities had antedated her decision to return to Europe.

To prevent Modotti's extradition from the Netherlands, the Dutch Left instructed a group of famous attorneys to make a request for political asylum on her behalf. In this way the government would have to confront the growing protests, but it was one step ahead, prohibiting Modotti from disembarking in Rotterdam. Italian pressure was increasingly insistent, and to grant her asylum now would have meant a diplomatic incident with Mussolini's government. After many bureaucratic vicissitudes, she was granted permission to go ashore on the condition that she leave the country that same day. The Dutch Communist Party received help from the German Communist Party, which interceded on her behalf, and she was issued a visa to enter Germany. On April 14, 1930, Modotti arrived in Berlin.

Vittorio Vidali had received orders to return to Moscow. He proposed that Modotti move to the Soviet Union with him. She refused. She needed time by herself before making such an irreversible decision.

Fourteen

If in Mexico Modotti had been able to enjoy some of the most intense events in that country's history, in Germany she arrived too late. In 1927 intellectual and artistic life had reached the peak of frenzy in a nation set on overcoming the defeat of its empire, but the 1929 Wall Street crisis devastated the German economy. In one year the creativity of literary Berlin, of Bauhaus architecture, and of musical and theatrical innovations fell quickly into oblivion because of the millions of unemployed beggars and panhandlers in search of food and shelter for the night. The obtuse politics of the victorious powers insisted on humiliating them further and imposing useless restrictions that nurtured the thirst for revenge. National Socialism grew on fertile ground, demonstrating the powerlessness of the four million Communist votes and their seventy-seven seats in the Reichstag.

Modotti admired the Berliners' tireless capacity for sacrifice, but in her journals she spoke of sad people without smiles, who walked through the streets serious and always in a hurry, as if reflecting the consciousness of an imminent tragedy:

*I have not seen the sun once during my ten days here, and for one com-
ing from Mexico the change is rather cruel. But I know that the wisest
thing is just to forget the sun, blue skies, and other delights of Mexico
and adapt myself to this new reality, and start, once more, life all over.*

In the Mexican capital Modotti and Weston had met a German couple, the Wittes, who had been their guests and who deeply admired the
work of the two photographers. In their correspondence with Modotti
they had repeatedly assured her that there would always be a room for
her in Berlin.

Even though she totally counted on these friends, she immediately
began to look for economic independence by using her professional experience. But the popularity of photography in Germany was greater than
in any other country, and therefore there was an abundance of photographers. Finding a paying job was anything but easy:

*The idea of portraiture in Berlin rather frightens me; there are so many
really excellent photographers here, and such an abundance of them,
both professional and amateur, and even the average work is excellent; I
mean even the work one sees in the windows along the street. . . . I have
been wondering if I could not work out a scheme by which to get a sort of
income from the blessed U.S. Perhaps by contributing to periodicals,
magazines, etc. I feel that if Frau Goldschmidt gets around one hundred
marks for articles in the* New York Times, *I should be able to do the same.*

And she asked Weston if he could help her through the German photographers whom he knew. This move revealed the enormous difficulties
that Modotti was facing, to the point of breaking a custom that was
deeply rooted in her:

*I well know it is not good policy to look up photographers if one is also a
photographer, but all I would want from them is practical advice as to
purchasing materials and finding a place to do some printing, etc. If possible I never again want to go to the trouble of fixing up a darkroom, and
I hope to be able to work in some darkroom. If I was in the U.S. I would
become a member of the photographers' association and make use of
their work rooms; perhaps something like that exists here. I shall see.*

And she added a postscript that underscored her semicladestine situation:

I must beg you to divulge as little as possible my presence here. It might cause me trouble in the future. Thanks!

Modotti seemed to have granted her creativity a temporary leave from her commitment of total dedication to the political mission. It would be the last.

Her meeting with Hannes Meyer marked the beginning of a close friendship that would survive all future tragedies. The architect had already fallen into disgrace, despite the dissolution of the Communist cell of the Bauhaus, of which he had been the director. Removed from his post, he left the prestigious school, now divided by political tensions.

Through Meyer, Modotti learned about the photographs of the masters who had been linked to the Bauhaus. Their work surprised her with innovative ideas it expressed. She contacted the Hungarian László Moholy-Nagy, who was doing experimental work on photograms with the Dutchman Piet Zwaart, who worked with collages and with the photomontage techniques of John Heartfield. She also studied the pictorial-photographic research of the Austrian Herbert Bayer and the Soviet Alexander Rodchenko. But despite her varied interests, Modotti remained on the margins, looking for an individual expressiveness that did not seem to exist in the Berlin environment. This was also due in part to Weston's aversion for Moholy-Nagy, which had reached its height at an exhibition of both their works in New York, where the American had been extremely critical of the Hungarian's experimentation.

The photos taken by Modotti conveyed an unforeseeable irony, in contrast to the somber climate in which she had been immersed for the last two years. It was as if for a brief period of time she had suddenly been freed from the populist rhetoric of her last Mexican photos, capturing the most absurd and caricature-like aspects of life in Berlin with a new sensibility, no doubt less dramatic but not superficial. In the dozen works that were saved from her continual moves, the luminous Modotti seemed to appear again, unbiased, inclined to play with her own life and with the lives of others, but without offending anyone, limiting herself to smiling to the side.

Difficulties on the technical level were not lacking either, as she had to adapt to the 35 mm Leica that everyone was now using in Germany and give up the large-format Graflex with which she was already familiar. On May 14, 1930, she joined the Unionfoto GMBH, an association of professional photographers, which furnished her with her reporter's credentials.

I have been offered to do "reportage" or newspaper work, but I feel not fitted for such work. I still think it is a man's work in spite of the fact that many women here do it; perhaps they can; I am not aggressive enough. Even the type of propaganda pictures I began to do in Mexico is already being done here; there is an association of "workers-photographers" (here everybody uses a camera), and the workers themselves make those pictures and indeed have better opportunities than I could ever have, since it is their own life and problems they photograph. Of course, their results are far from the standard I am struggling to keep up in photography, but the end is reached just the same.

I feel there must be something for me but I have not found it yet. And in the meantime the days go by and I spend sleepless nights wondering which way to turn and where to begin. I have begun to go out with the camera, but nada.

This time she asked Weston not to write her name on the envelope of future letters, which were delivered to the Wittes. The political situation was accelerating into a spiral of persecutions and armed confrontations. Nazi ideology was winning over the masses, gaining seven million votes in September 1930. Modotti's difficulties could only intensify in the face of the emergence of a dictatorship that was not based on passiveness but rather on the eager involvement of the majority of Germans—their frustrations, which generated irrational explosions of violence, and the desperate reaction to the economic disaster of the Weimar Republic. And yet there were still moments of enthusiasm, recorded by sudden changes in tone in her letters to Weston:

A few days ago I wrote to you again but now I almost regret having sent it; I was in such a despondent state of mind and weak enough to not just keep it to myself and made you the victim of my weakness. Please forgive

*me, and do not worry about me; I will fight my way and the last word
has not been said yet, and all these trials will bear some fruit, I am sure;
in other words, I have enough self-confidence and realize I must not un-
dervalue my capacities. Only there are moments, who doesn't have them?
when everything appears black (perhaps they are black and those are
the moments of lucidity) but maybe the next day the sun shines and the
little birds sing, and the panorama changes as if by magic!*

The absence of the warmth of Mexico had a profound influence on
her moods. Her work was also affected by her difficulties in adapting:

*I was interested in your decision about the glossy paper. Yes, I can just
picture the "pictorials" lifting their arms in horror at this new "outrage"
by this terrible, terrible iconoclast Edward Weston! So far I have under-
timed everything I began to make; this damned light after Mexico! And
yet I had accounted for it; but I will know better in the future!*

She did not take long to prove that statement. The photographer
Lotte Jacobi mounted Modotti's work in a private exhibition in her studio, provoking great emotion in the critic Egon Erwin Kisch, who would
later write:

Her secret lies in managing to reflect a vision of reality through her image
of the world. That means that she succeeds in making the sad eyes of a
child more beautiful than the eyes of a little queen. And the industrial
landscapes, the means of production, the hands, the guitars—look more
fascinating than the green trails of Switzerland. But the men in her world
are not happy. Why? That is the question one senses in her photographs.

Kisch's reference to the "green trails of Switzerland" may have referred to one of Modotti's photographs that would later be cataloged as
"German countryside." But on the outskirts of Berlin there was no area
that resembled the green valley with forests of fir trees and typical Swiss
chalets. The photo was probably taken during a secret trip on behalf of
Red Aid. A letter sent from Switzerland to her Mexican friend Baltazar
Dromundo proved that Tina made this trip. A leader of the student movement and a friend of Mella, Dromundo felt a deep affection for Modotti

that probably at some point turned into love. A few months before leaving Mexico, Modotti had given him a photo of herself, taken by Weston, with the following dedication:

> Baltasar—no words could better express than the look on this face the sadness and pain I feel at not being able to give life to all the marvelous possibilities I envision. The seeds of which already exist and only await the "sacred fire" which should emanate from me but which when I look for it, I find it extinguished. Allow me to use the word *defeat* in this case. I will tell you that I feel defeated for having nothing else to offer and for "having no more energy for affection." I have to admit this, I, who have always given so much of myself.

Modotti's trip to Switzerland seemed to have escaped the surveillance of Italian counterespionage. But OVRA kept looking incessantly for her trail, mobilizing the many informants who had infiltrated the Italian community. A certain Chief Police Inspector Accomando was appointed by the embassy to keep an eye on the activities of the Italian subversives who resided in Berlin. A report from June 3, 1930, read:

> From the information gathered by Police Inspector Accomando in those circles that are normally interested in Communist photographic exhibitions, it has not been concluded, at least as of today, that an exhibition of Mexican photos is being organized. While the investigation continues, we have informed the local police through Accomando of the probable presence of the dangerous Communist Modotti in Berlin.

Fortunately for Modotti, she did not take part in public exhibitions and did not frequent Berlin's Italian circles. This also explained why Accomando would not discover her residence in the Schulz Pension at 5 Tauentzienstrasse until many months later, when she was already very far away.

The success she had begun to have with her work was not enough to keep her in Germany. For a few months photography had crept back into her life and reawakened the energy that remained from a passion that, in any case, had become secondary. Unable to express her ideas openly, she was forced to limit her discussions to the homes of her friends. For the

Germans, Communist militancy now translated into underground work that responded to Nazi aggressions with one blow after another. Modotti realized in an increasingly painful way the lack of an atmosphere that she would never be able to find in Europe. Vidali showed up for short periods, and he always tried to persuade her to go with him to Moscow. Finally, with her six-month residency permit about to expire, Modotti had no choice. Before leaving the German capital she went to see Leo Matthias, who did not know she was in the city and was very surprised when he saw her. During the afternoon she spent at his house, Modotti told him about her latest internal conflicts, about her separation from Weston, and about her intention of moving to Moscow. Matthias tried to dissuade her, warning her about the worsening political situation in the Soviet Union and the climate of tension that had come about after Trotsky's deportation. She did not respond, as if her decision were irrevocable.

> The streets were already deserted when I accompanied her to her hotel late that night. Only the echoes of our footsteps could be heard. We exchanged very few words, walking slowly, as if we were following the funeral of an invisible casket.

Modotti left Berlin, as well as photography, in October 1930. An era was over. But in fleeing the sinister echoes of a Europe gone mad, she would confront the silent tragedy of her repressed and betrayed ideas.

Part Four

CROSSING BORDERS

Fifteen

Five months before Modotti arrived in Moscow, Vladimir Maya-kovsky had taken his final sheet of paper and written: "As they say, the incident is settled. The raft of love has crashed into everyday life. And with life I am now even." Then he shot a bullet through his heart.

But for Modotti, who was coming from a rootless and lonely situation, Moscow represented the protective security of an environment that took her in, offering her the first stability of her life. At first everything seemed grandiose and involved to her, an immense workshop in which every cog was working to build a new world. The Party assigned her a room, which she would share with Vidali, in the Hotel Soyuznaya, where all the officials stayed. Their reunion was no longer hindered by security measures or by limitations of secrecy. However, they did not take into account the strict Bolshevik morality in Moscow, of which Elena Stasova, Lenin's former secretary and now Stalin's, was the unyielding enforcer.

Stasova called Vidali to her office, from which she exercised much more extensive powers than those of a mere associate of the supreme leader, and reprimanded him severely for his immoral conduct: In fact, his relationship with Paulina Hafkina was not over, and his on-again off-again relationship with Tina Modotti was a symptom of a lack of morality that was entirely at odds with the socialist ethic. Vidali denied that his relationship with Modotti was anything other than common political work, and he stated that he was expecting a child with Hafkina. A few days later Blanca was born, defusing Stasova's suffocating scrutiny. Immediately after the child's birth, he "officially" separated from his acknowledged companion and was able to stay on at the Soyuznaya without incurring the wrath of the moralistic secretary.

Modotti also had an issue to clear up with respect to her personal relationships. She tried to contact Xavier Guerrero, as she felt the need to explain to him personally what she had written in her letter. But he avoided any contact with her, had people tell her that he was not in, and did not respond to the messages she left for him at the Hotel Lux, where he was staying. Finally she decided to wait for him outside the door to his room.

When Guerrero found her there he was unmoved. The man who in Mexico had been called "the statue of rock" seemed to have heightened his characteristic impenetrability even more. He showed no reaction, not even a hello or an expression of surprise. He let her in, but he just stood in the middle of the room with his arms crossed, staring at her, expressionless. Modotti talked to him about the letter and about how hard it had been for her to write it; she tried hard to explain to him that she had had no choice, that it was the only way to not deceive him. And she asked him if, in spite of everything, they could be friends, hoping that he could overcome the ill will he bore her.

Guerrero, silent and solemn as always, watched her without moving a single muscle.

"I'm begging you, Xavier," Modotti implored, "at least say something."

He slowly headed toward the door and opened it. Modotti looked straight at him, shaking helplessly, and she understood that dialogue was no longer possible. Resigned, she made her way to the door. When she was in the doorway he muttered very softly, "There is nothing worth discussing. You should have known that. As far as I'm concerned, we never met."

Modotti reacted impulsively and tried to go over to him, but she was paralyzed by his icy stare. She swallowed several times to hold back the tears that were about to fall and shook her head without finding any words to break through the wall that separated them. She took a few steps toward the corridor and turned to wave good-bye. Guerrero threw his head back slightly and said, "I found out that you are with the Italian."

She opened her mouth, but before she could say anything he added, "If there really were another world, I would like to see Julio's face right now."

Modotti shrank, as if she had just felt an unbearable, intense pain. Guerrero looked at her with contempt and closed the door silently.

On November 7 Modotti took part in the commemorative demonstration of the October Revolution. There were masses of red flags, the ground in the immense square shook under the avalanche of crowds converging from all directions. The thrilling atmosphere was full of brass bands and choruses, shouting and incitements, mottoes and thunderous applause. Vittorio Vidali was next to Modotti, and he was greeted by important people from the Party and the army. Stalin had shaken his hand for the first time in 1928. When they invited him to the platform, the "little father" looked at him with a solemn smile. For Modotti the emotions of that day were the confirmation that she had chosen the right path.

Assigned to the foreign office of Red Aid, she immersed herself with tireless discipline in bureaucratic work. Her knowledge of several languages and the dedication that kept her holed up in her office twelve hours a day earned her a kind of promotion to the department of press and propaganda. She translated foreign newspaper articles and took charge of the archives, but she also wrote reports and declarations, and they sent her to factories to give lectures on repression in European and Latin American countries.

Her initial enthusiasm was reflected in a letter she wrote to Weston in December 1930:

I have been living in a regular whirlpool ever since I came here in October; so much so that I cannot even remember whether I have written to

you or not since my arrival. But at any rate, today I received the an-
nouncement for your exhibit (just three months later due to the careless-
ness of the person who forwards my mail in Berlin), and I cannot wait
one day longer to send you saludos *with the same feeling of always! I*
have never had less time for myself than right now; this has its advan-
tages—but also drawbacks, the main one being the utter lack of time to
devote to you, for instance, if only through a few badly scribbled words.
There would be so much to write about life here but no hay tiempo*—I am*
living a completely new life, so much so that I almost feel like a different
person, but very interesting. . . . Dear Edward, if ever you feel you are in
the mood for a few words to me, the Berlin address is still good, only if
possible, write compact, for many reasons.

But her relationship with Weston ended there, with those few words.
It was Modotti's last letter. After January 12, 1931, the day he received
it, Weston would never hear from her again.

An unbridgeable gulf now separated them; Modotti had put her
doubts aside, and that "whirlwind of events" translated into an absolute
faith that did not allow looking back. For a while her letters were mono-
logues between two people who had only the memory of the past in common. She did not attempt to convince him of her ideals, but nor did she
conceal the emotions she was experiencing. In some cases she wrote him
to let off steam, because with no other man would she have been able to
reveal the anguish she felt about what was going on around her, or her
hope of a brighter future. In the meantime, his pessimism about hu-
mankind had been turning into a visceral intolerance for anything that
had to do with "the masses."

Vidali's presence had also had an effect on Weston, at least in part.
For Vidali it was inconceivable that Modotti was still involved with an
"individualistic bourgeois" who displayed an obvious aversion for Communism. And he missed no occasion to remind her that the Soviet Union,
having to defend itself from all kinds of enemies, internal as well as ex-
ternal, was obliged to subtly control the relationships of foreign militants.

Photo sent to her mother in 1920 when Tina was an actress in silent films.

Tina at four years old.

Section of a Diego Rivera mural in which Tina distributes weapons to the insurgents.

Tina Modotti in the movie *The
Tiger's Coat*, filmed in Hollywood
in 1920.

Drawing of Tina by
Diego Rivera, 1926.

Tina and Roubaix de l'Abrie Richey "Robo" at their home in Los Angeles.

Portrait of Edward Weston by Tina Modotti, 1923.

Tina posing nude for Edward Weston on the roof terrace of her house in Mexico City, 1924.

Vittorio Vidali, the *comandante* Carlos, in 1932.

Tina's police record in Italy.

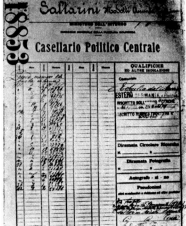

Young Communist leader Julio
Antonio Mella, photographed
by Tina in 1928.

Tina's grave, with poetry by
Pablo Neruda, in the Dolores
Cemetery, Mexico City.

Photographs by Tina Modotti

Guitar, Bandolier, and Sickle. TINA MODOTTI, 1927.

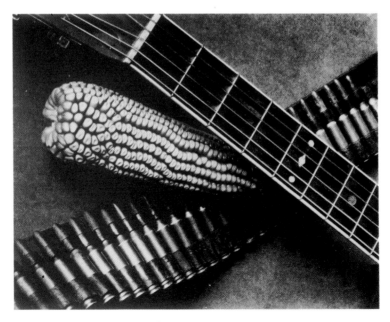

Bandolier, Ear of Corn, and Guitar. TINA MODOTTI, 1928.

Arches in Convent with Stairs. TINA MODOTTI, 1924.

Worker's Hands with Shovel. TINA MODOTTI, 1926.

Peasant Reading El Machete. TINA MODOTTI, 1927.

Julio Antonio Mella's Typewriter. TINA MODOTTI, 1929.

Telegraph Wires. TINA MODOTTI, 1923.

Woman from Tehuantepec. TINA MODOTTI, 1928.

Woman with Flag. TINA MODOTTI, 1927.

Woman from Tehuantepec Carrying Baby. TINA MODOTTI, 1929.

Calla Lilies. TINA MODOTTI, 1927.

Sixteen

Political and economic pressures had the Soviet Union in a stranglehold, but that should not have been enough to justify the paranoid involution that was destroying, one after another, the victories of independence and autonomy. "All power to the Soviets"—that is to say, to the representative councils—was now the motto of a romantic past, erased by a reality in which any decision was the result of shady plots and related strategies. The political climate was becoming increasingly rigid. The enormous effort to carry out the first Five-Year Plan showed the other face of the "revolution in a single country." Poverty, weariness, and sadness in the people who were dragged along by the force of inertia, searching for a reason to keep believing, while they passively witnessed the growth of the bureaucratic leviathan, of the octopus-tentacled informer willing to denounce the smallest infraction of Stalinist orthodoxy.

Vidali was one of the few foreigners who had a Party membership card, a sign of the great confidence that the Party had in him. But in 1933, like all militants and officials, he had to pass through the filter of the Central Committee's CISKA, the official organization that made decisions regarding purges. A commission of the Central Committee conducted an exhaustive study of the biographical data, and only if it was proved that these data were totally free from suspicion of "hypocrisy" and "degeneration of petit bourgeois origin" would the card be returned. Vidali had the unpleasant surprise of facing Luigi Longo in the role of accuser; Longo did not hesitate to denounce him for his past "terrorist inclinations." But the "comrade president" of CISKA rose personally to his defense, praising his integrity as an honorable militant. The services rendered by Vidali probably protected him from any attempt by Party comrades from Italy to denounce him.

Modotti continued to participate in all executive committee meetings and in the activity of the Party cell she had joined, progressively closing herself up in a passive silence. She refused to get involved in the controversies about "Trotskyism" and "Bukharinism," and she attended all the discussions about the different "deviationisms" without opening her mouth. When she too had to appear before CISKA, she was asked if she was in complete agreement with the Party line; she responded with a simple yes, adding nothing more.

"**D**o you see? Do you understand what this means for me?"

Vidali shouted, leaning forward and shaking his fists, clenching them until his knuckles were white. The veins in his neck and forehead were throbbing, swollen by the rage he was venting in the semidark room. He abruptly moved toward the small table in the corner and poured himself another glass of vodka from an unlabeled bottle, a very strong, cheap alcohol. Modotti looked up.

"Stop it already. You are waking up at least three floors of the hotel."

He seemed to freeze. He stared at her, his eyes red, suddenly looking hurt, disillusioned.

"So then you don't understand. Not even you have understood anything about what has really happened!"

Modotti got up and went to take a cigarette from the pack that was sticking out of the pocket of her heavy wool coat. Exhaling the smoke, she said quietly, "Yes, yes. But how many times have you told me it's not necessary to explain anything?"

Vidali threw his hair back and took a deep breath to calm himself down.

"Okay, okay, you're right. I'm making quite a scene, and maybe . . . someone is listening on the other side of the wall. But I at least thought I had the help of a friend. For me, Longo was a friend!"

His voice became hoarse, and the sentence ended in a muted gurgle.

"A friend—and he nearly had me thrown out of the Party. Do you understand what that means for me?"

He turned to look straight at her, with a look of amazement that slowly turned into overwhelming certainty. He had not realized the extent to which she had become hardened, masked in a cloak of iciness.

"Tina, he denounced me. Longo denounced me, one of the few *compañeros* I could count on . . . and you . . . don't you have anything else to say? Anything else to—"

"You should have expected it, Vittorio. A few years ago you taught me that all this forms part of what you call 'class struggle,' right? And you have used it when you thought it appropriate to eliminate certain obstacles along the way. I am only repeating your words. Now you seem shocked, only because for a moment you found yourself in the place of those who suffer from the rules instead of impose them."

"What the devil are you talking about? That swine called me 'a terrorist' in front of the commission! He could have destroyed me!"

Modotti opened her arms and smiled ambiguously.

"In order to destroy you, more is needed than Luigi Longo's word. In the end you have come out stronger. The 'comrade president' has praised the service you have provided the Comintern. Everyone has confirmed your loyalty. What more do you want?"

She took a long drag on her cigarette while he continued pacing and sipping his drink nervously.

Operative agent Vittorio Vidali was too useful to the Party to risk losing his services as the result of some vague accusations about his "terrorist inclinations." His work in Moscow consisted primarily of controlling the Club of Italian Emigrants, a circle that for some time had voiced criticism of the international political decisions imposed by Stalin. There were 226 Italian Communists who set out on the one-way road to Siberia, another 9 were executed in the courtyards of the secret prisons, 4 committed suicide, and 2 died in a mental hospital.

Headquarters was in a small old palace that had belonged to a landowner until the October Revolution. In the entrance, a marble plaque commemorated the "counterrevolutionary" attack carried out on the premises on September 25, 1919, when anarchists threw a bomb at the secretary of the committee, Vladimir Zagorsky, in protest at the persecutions of Bolsheviks. There was a hall for gatherings that looked like a theater with a stage, another one for the assemblies of national sessions, an office with a secretary for each delegation, and a bar open from six in the evening until midnight.

The president of the club—who was immediately nicknamed "the Stalinist robot" by some of the future convicts—was Paolo Robotti, brother-in-law of Italian Communist Party leader Palmiro Togliatti. Giovanni Germanetto, Clarenzo Menotti, and Vittorio Vidali were named his "advisers." Modotti also frequented the clubs but she did so without revealing her presence.

After Robotti's appointment, decided in a meeting of the Italian delegation of the Comintern, presided over by Togliatti, the new "directives" on the identification of "deviationists" created a climate of mutual distrust and suspicion. All the Communists who gathered there to debate had been saved from fascist tribunals and had arrived in Moscow carrying in their hearts the hope of being able to take part in the building of a new world. But the naive view of the social system that they had so often dreamed about contrasted harshly with everything before their eyes. Their conversations were monitored closely by officials who feigned understanding and indifference, prepared to report any restlessness, including the slightest hint of criticism. Emilio Guarnaschelli found himself among those Communists who had passed from initial enthusiasm for Soviet society to disillusion about the injustices and the aberrant climate of oppression, whose victim he would become through the denunciation of a false friend willing to listen to his venting. He perished in a gulag, never knowing the real reasons for his being accused as a "traitor."

Robotti, availing himself of his loyal advisers, possessed a detailed notebook from which accusations arose. In self-criticism sessions, everyone had to recite his mea culpa, recalling even the most insignificant "error" committed in the past. Many preferred to invent small forgivable mistakes instead of remaining silent before the commission. In any case there was always something to defend oneself against in that small but endless notebook.

Seventeen

Silent, despondent, and engulfed in impenetrable gloom, Modotti continued working as a translator and patiently filing away articles and analyses. Perhaps precisely to flee that asphixiating climate, she offered to go on risky missions abroad. From 1932 to 1933, she traveled to Poland, Hungary, and Romania, working for Red Aid. She also spent short periods of time in Spain, where the police finally detained her. Her fake passport, which identified her this time as a citizen of Guatemala, did not pass the thorough immigration controls, and she was deported on suspicion of belonging to the Soviet services. Her next mission was in Vienna, where she took part in the insurrection against the dictatorship of Chancellor Engelbert Dollfuss.

In August 1933 Modotti and Vidali were called to the Fourth Section of the Red Army, headquarters of the military secret service. Gen. Jan Karlovic Berzin, in charge of counter-espionage, explained to them a delicate mission that was still in the planning phase: They would travel to China and infiltrate Richard Sorge's network, and Modotti would play a fundamental role because of her knowledge of photography and her facility with languages. They accepted.

Sorge would go down in history as the Soviet spy who in 1941 provided the date of the imminent German attack. Stalin did not want to assemble troops on the border for fear of giving their Nazi ally a pretext to invade, as he thought that any provocation would alarm Hitler. He even told his closest advisers to verify the loyalty of whoever tried to warn him. At 3:15 in the morning on June 22, 1941, three units of the German army crossed Soviet lines and advanced toward Leningrad, Kiev, Kharkov, and Moscow. In December of that same year, they were stopped by the harsh winter and by the sacrifice of the best men in the Red Army. Stalin took advantage of the opportunity to eliminate a number of high officials who would soon have become a danger to him, constructing at the same time the epic resistance to the invaders, which would further justify his punishment of the traitors. Sorge paid with his life for his useless risk: Discovered by the Japanese, he was sentenced to be hanged.

A few days before Modotti and Vidali were to depart, Stasova blocked the mission. The order was signed by Kliment Voroshilov, commander in chief of the Soviet armed forces. The fact remained that in August 1933, Tina Modotti agreed to enter the military secret service. The reason for the sudden cancellation of the mission was not known.

For several months in 1934, Modotti lived in Paris, where Vidali would join her. To avoid a second "incident" after everything that had happened in Spain, they were forced to live in secrecy. She used a Costa Rican passport, and under no circumstances could she allow herself to be identified as an emissary sent by Moscow to organize the foreign center of Red Aid. She and Vidali lived apart and saw each other every now and then in public, taking care to avoid police checkpoints. In fact, it was Vidali who could not allow himself to be identified. Crossing borders and passing through the secret service networks of dozens of countries was his specialty, and among the countless files that were accumulating on him, no two had the same name. Each file contained different personal data and a different citizenship, which therefore made it impossible to know which one was authentic.

But in spite of the precautions they both took, one night Vidali realized that he was being followed. He was headed for the apartment that was used as an archive for the records of Red Aid in France, where Tina was waiting for him to put the finishing touches on a series of interventions ordered by Moscow. The house looked like a private residence; meetings were not held there, and only two or three militants visited it at a time.

Vidali noticed that at least two men had been tailing him since he had gotten off the last bus. Evidently, despite many transfers, he had not succeeded in losing them. There were probably many others, and they took turns following him. Vidali's instinct had saved him in many similar situations, putting him on guard before it was too late. But this time he recognized that he was dealing with professionals, and the idea of running down a back alley had proved futile on at least two occasions. They always caught him farther ahead, a sign that the whole area that he was traversing was already under surveillance. He would need a car in order to get out of the neighborhood quickly, or even to leave Paris and then warn Modotti, so she could destroy all the files and run. But even then he might not escape. If they had chosen such a deployment of forces, they would also surely have cars ready at a distance.

Vidali touched the butt of his pistol, but his hand immediately slipped off because of the cold sweat that was also running down his back and face. He had to get rid of them. He now had no escape, and to be caught with a weapon on him could imperil him irreparably. Defending himself was crazy. There were too many; they would kill him without giving him time to attack more than one, at the most two, of them. And if they wounded him . . . He ran his hand across his eyes to wipe away the sweat that clouded his vision. He imagined the headlines in the newspapers, the international incident, the problems of the Soviet government . . . They would get rid of him for jeopardizing the work of many of his comrades, something that would condemn him to the limbo of other ruined operative agents, without the slightest possibility of returning to Moscow.

The pavement was slippery from the heavy spring rain that had fallen a few hours before. Jumping over a puddle, he fell flat on his face, cursing out loud. He faked having twisted his ankle and rolled over on his side, and as he did he threw his pistol behind some garbage cans. He got up angrily and began to walk, limping. Two headlights appeared across the street, and the brightness paralyzed him momentarily. It was a taxi. He raised his arm and ran toward it, but the car swerved, avoiding him, and sped off, only giving him time to make out the figure in the backseat, and he mumbled a curse.

The grip on his arm was like a vise, but the voice was strangely pleasant.

"Enough now. No more foolishness."

The man smiled and made a gesture, inviting him to follow, while the other one searched him quickly. A third man appeared from the other side of the street, and a dark car soon appeared at the end of the street.

"What do you want? Who are you?" he asked, looking both terrified and astonished.

The man holding his arm stuck his other hand under his jacket. He pulled out a metal badge that shone under the street lamp.

"Deuxième Bureau. Come with us, please. We just want to exchange views with you briefly."

The room was immersed in darkness, with the exception of a massive dark mahogany desk, illuminated by a greenish lamp that gave off a diffuse light. It did not look like a counterespionage office, much less a basement used for interrogations. But the refined way in which it was furnished and that absurd bronze lamp, with the twisted figure of a winged nymph holding a heavy shell of thick, swollen glass, made the atmosphere even more sinister. Vidali was surprised by their friendliness, by the absence of bad manners and threats, and even by the pictures on the walls that did not depict fathers of the homeland but rather were drawings of the city from bygone eras, images of crowds spread out along barricades and faces of women inciting the attack of a fortress in flames.

"As you can see, we have some experience when it comes to revolutions."

The voice was hoarse, with a touch of sarcasm. Vidali turned around after a few seconds, controlling his instinct to jump from his chair. He was a man of about forty, younger than what he had imagined from the tired tone and breathlessness. He walked around him, observing him from head to toe with a smile of complicity. He pointed to a print framed in red wood and murmured, "Barricades, smoke, open mouths—the motivations and ideals can change, but the one thing that remains the same is the smell of blood."

He went to sit in an armchair in the corner, forcing Vidali to turn around and look at him from an uncomfortable position.

"And then, as the years go by, everyone begins to ask themselves if it was really worth it."

Vidali was motionless. He held his gaze without showing any emotion, waiting for the first question.

"You, on the other hand, are one of those who believe in the absolute originality of your own experiences, isn't that right?"

Vidali made an almost imperceptible expression with his lips, a vague look of smugness, and after a few seconds said, "I believe only that you have the wrong person."

The man shrugged, dismissing with his hand what he considered to be a waste of time.

"I didn't have you brought here so you could invent plausible justifications, much less to hear excuses. You, sir—by the way, what do you prefer to be called?"

Vidali pointed to his passport, which was on the desk.

"It's written right there. I am an Uruguayan citizen and my name is—"

"Yes, it's first-rate work," he interrupted, "I don't doubt the talent of the forgers at your disposal. I only want to know to what extent that is worthy of consideration."

And he got up to open a drawer of the filing cabinet and took out a paper that he brought to the light so he could read.

"Sormenti, Enea, or Contreras, Carlos, believed to be Vittorio Vidali, son of Giovanni and Bianca Rizzi, from Muggia, Trieste, born on March 3, 1901, object of a previous communiqué, etc.—"

He stopped to look sharply at him, noting that the OVRA report did not produce the slightest reaction from him. He nodded, sighing with a resigned look.

"Mr. Vidali, neither one of us has time to waste. And in the end we perform the same work. Governments and ideals change, become transformed, switch around, but people like you and me always remain in their position, because no power can do without us."

He put the paper back in the drawer.

"Don't you think so?"

"I can guess what your occupation is, but it surely has nothing to do with mine," Vidali rebuffed dryly.

"It's fine if you've decided to play your role beyond reasonable limits, so continue if you like. I only wanted to inform you that my country is willing to tolerate your presence, but it will not permit any interference in French internal matters."

He went over to the desk and rested his hands on top of it. He seemed to have given up any attempt to appear cordial.

"In other words, carry on with your control work and reporting. Your revenge does not interest us. But I am warning you: If you have received orders to eliminate some unfortunate person on behalf of the government you are currently depending on, we will be forced to prevent you from doing so. We don't want anything like that to occur on French soil. Have I made myself clear?"

Vittorio opened his arms and smiled faintly. "As for making yourself clear—yes, you were perfectly clear. What a pity that I am not the man you think I am."

"If by that you mean that there is a difference between the Deuxième Bureau and the GPU, you are right to a certain extent, but it is merely superficial. The principle is the same."

Vidali stood up suddenly.

"If there is a warrant for my arrest, show it to me. If not, I demand—"

"Please, spare me the big scene, and calm down, because nobody intends to arrest you. Of course . . . Your back is well covered, Mr. Vidali, and we do not want problems with the Soviet government. I am just doing you the favor of inviting you to leave France as soon as possible. Act accordingly."

"I hope I won't see you again," the man who was now pretending to look over some files added dryly.

Vidali turned and walked toward the wide-open door.

"Ah, one last thing."

Vidali stopped and turned to look at him, but the man did not look up. He was bent over a drawer, from which he removed the pistol Vidali had thrown away in the street.

"I'm sorry, but we have to keep this one." He smiled with a look of false regret.

"Unfortunately, the registration numbers are scratched off, and you know how the bureaucracy is. But I'm sure you won't have any problems getting them to provide you with a new one. The main thing"—he looked up, holding the pistol with his fingertips—"is that you avoid using it here. Take it as a piece of advice, *colleague to colleague.*"

Vidali stared at the weapon, not knowing if he should reply.

"I'm counting on your discretion. Good-bye forever, Mr. Carlos Contreras."

Two hours had passed since their scheduled meeting, and that car was still parked at the head of the alley across the street. Now Modotti was sure that something had happened to Vidali. What upset her even more was the complete lack of precautions of the two men down there, who did nothing to hide themselves. The apartment was being watched in too obvious a way, as if they wanted to provoke a reaction in order to move in. She put out her cigarette in the ashtray and stopped for a moment to count the cigarettes she had smoked nonstop.

She had no other choice. She quickly went over to the woodstove, opened the little door, and quickly went back and dumped out the drawers in the middle of the room, frantic. When she had emptied them all, she stood staring at the heap of papers thrown on the floor. Then she began to stick them by the handful into the stove, stuffing it until the fire was smothered. She cursed the slowness with which the paper burned, and she cursed that damn stove that couldn't manage to destroy the thousands of names, reports, analyses, predictions, and records of long-time enemies and recent "traitors." The smoke gushed forth, spreading out at the ceiling, and then came down in an increasingly thick fog that did not allow her to breathe or to see. She covered her mouth with a handkerchief and continued throwing papers inside, where from time to time a flame would spring up. She coughed, and the tears could no longer alleviate the burning in her eyes.

Suddenly she heard a noise behind her, nervous steps; somebody bumped into a chair that hit the wall. Instinctively Tina seized the large tongs for turning over the coals and, when she turned around, disoriented, she staggered and fell to her knees, groping in the smoke that was paralyzing her lungs. She saw the friendly face of an old German comrade and felt some hands lift her up and drag her toward the window, which was opened wide with a sharp blow. Then she was dragged toward the door and moved to the landing; the door was closed and she felt her throat inflamed by the oxygen she inhaled in small breaths, trying to overcome the vise that was squeezing her chest.

After a few minutes Willy Koska went back inside and finished burning the files little by little. Tina went back into the room, where the smoke was now reduced to a stagnant blue veil on the ceiling. He too had gone there to destroy the files, and now he scolded her kindly for the risk she had taken. Tina was bent over in a chair, staring vacantly at him.

Vidali arrived later. The joy of seeing him again, alive and free, lasted just long enough for her to listen to the brief explanation of his detention. Modotti felt an uncontrollable rage rise up inside of her, a pent-up resentment toward that man who kept risking his life and used that contemptuous tone, almost boasting of having escaped unharmed once again. And when he criticized her for having acted in such a rash way, accusing her of losing control in the face of an emergency, she got up and began to insult him.

"Do you think the whole world is like you, without any kind of feelings when it comes time to respond and act and if anyone gets lost along the way, so much the better! I mean that wasn't important enough, isn't that it? And I, the idiot on duty, worrying. . . . About what, then? I should have known that the courageous Comrade Vidali always works things out!"

"Tina, control yourself. You know you shouldn't use my name under any circumstances."

"You see? I am just a hysterical little woman who threatens to ruin the missions of the uncatchable, unnamable comrade! And if I had suffocated you would have filled out your excellent report reassuring the Party that, fortunately, you were there to fix everything."

"You are saying such nonsense that I prefer to forget it right now."

"Thank you, *compañero!* Thank you for not denouncing me for being distrustful in one of those cowardly, dirty reports of yours."

Vidali grabbed her by the wrists and shook her violently, forcing her to sit down.

"Shut up! You're exaggerating. We'll talk about it again when you've calmed down. You don't know what you're saying right now."

"You're the one who doesn't know what you're saying," she mumbled in a hoarse voice and with tears rolling down her soot-stained face. "You only know how to judge and categorize, and whoever makes a mistake you set aside, without ever stopping a moment to think—without ever asking yourself if that really is the only solution for everything."

"I don't even know what you're talking about. And we don't have time to lose. This house is being watched, and we have to inform our comrades so they stay away."

Modotti smiled faintly, sadly, looking at him with pity.

"There was a time when your certainty gave me strength. I clung to it like a rope in order to let myself be pulled from the mud. But now it just seems like a screen to hide your weakness. You lack the courage to suffer, Carlos. Your lack of doubts is just a desire not to see and not to feel."

"Be brief. What the hell do you want? Spit out whatever you have inside and do it quickly, because by now I should have already crossed the border."

"Crossed the border?"

"Yes, I'm going to Belgium tonight. If I stay here they'll probably arrest me. And they would organize a campaign around it that absolutely must be avoided."

He went over to her with his arms folded, provocatively.

"So? May I know what the problem is?"

Tina made a movement with her head, sighed, and shrank from a coughing attack that caused a sharp pain in her chest. "Nothing. There is no problem. For three days you've given no signs of life, and even without the French counterespionage, you would have arrived late anyway, not caring about how I might feel, that I spent hours hoping that you are in some bed and not in a jail cell."

Vidali turned away, impatient, and shook his hands saying, "Again the same stupidity! Now it appears I'm having a great time in this shitty city!"

"Don't delude yourself. I am not having a jealous fit. Those days are over. And I know very well the 'sacrifices' you have to make in order to establish contacts and expand operations."

"It was clear from the beginning that we weren't going to be able to see each other often here in Paris. Don't make me repeat the thousands of reasons that you know better than I."

"Only the Central Committee is better than you, and everyone else is just a mass of pawns that must be moved according to demands and orders."

Vidali shrugged, breathing heavily. He went to inspect the stove to verify that there were no legible papers left. Then he headed toward the door and, before opening it, stopped to say, "I'll send you news as soon as I find a job in Belgium. Use only the contact you know, and if everything goes well, he will tell you what to do in order to join me."

Eighteen

The assassination of Sergei Mironovich Kostricov (Kirov), the first secretary of the Soviet Communist Party in Leningrad, marked the culmination of the purging mania.

The Party's seventeenth Congress, held at the end of January 1934, would go down in history as the "Congress of the Victors." Praising the successes of the first Five-Year Plan and of the forced collectivizations in the countryside, it set forth an ambitious program for the immediate future. Despite an apparent unanimity of opinion, the more popular Party leaders, such as Kirov, Petrovsky, and Postyshev, were formulating a plan to remove Stalin from his post as secretary general. Once they took this position, many delegates voted against him. The attempt failed, however, and Stalin retreated even more into his strange conviction that he was surrounded by traitors. He even felt abandoned by the advisers whom he had placed in the highest posts, and who now realized the need to stop the monstrous mechanism that they themselves were nourishing.

Stalin spent the entire year of 1934 reinforcing his own personal power, adopting a series of countermeasures aimed at eliminating most of the officials who were by his side. In the middle of the year, he began a new series of purges, characterized by a meticulous inspection of the past lives of all Party members and by the collection of corresponding information, charging a few of his most loyal men to gather hundreds of thousands of dossiers. These files would spark the most indiscriminate and ruthless purges in Soviet history. However, Stalin wanted to avoid the risk of upsetting the delicate and very complicated balance, which would result if he accused the most charismatic figures; he knew and feared the influence these men had on the masses. He achieved his objective with Kirov, obtaining two important results: the elimination of a feared adversary and a *casus belli* to increase the repression even more.

On December 1, 1934, the young Communist militant Leonid Nikolayev walked through the door of the Smolny Palace in Leningrad and, without any guard from the strict security service stopping him, reached Kirov's office and opened fire on him with his regulation Nagant rifle.

Nikolayev had previously been detained and arrested at least twice by Kirov's personal bodyguard. In both cases inexplicable "superior orders" had freed him. Borisov, the man responsible for protecting Stalin, denounced the action to the investigating committee. But on the day set for his deposition, Borisov was captured by a group of military men in a van who wielded iron bars instead of rifles. About a hundred meters ahead, the van suddenly swerved and smashed into a wall. It was a minor accident and no one was injured, but Borisov died at once, his skull shattered "due to the impact."

When Nikolayev was brought before the same commission to state the motives that had led him to murder Kirov, he suddenly looked at the GPU officials who were present and shouted, "They forced me to do it! Ask them why!" The men at whom he was pointing immediately threw themselves on him and beat him with the butts of their guns until they broke his skull. After that day Nikolayev disappeared into thin air. He probably died in his jail cell without ever regaining consciousness.

A few hours after Kirov's death, Stalin, on behalf of the Central Committee, wrote the sadly famous letter on the lessons that were to be learned from the abominable assassination of their comrade Kirov.

We must stop the opportunistic naïveté derived from the enormous as-sumptions that, as our forces grow, the enemy becomes increasingly calm and innocuous. Such an assumption is completely wrong. It is a return of the deviationism of the right, which assured everyone, everywhere that the enemies would slip, without commotion, toward socialism.

We must remember that the more desperate the enemy's situation be-comes, the more they will resort to extreme measures as the only resort for people destined to die in the fight against Soviet power. We must re-member this and be constantly on guard.

A large crowd gathered to pay its last respects to Kirov. Modotti was a mere dot amid the ocean of bodies that vigorously applauded Stalin, en-couraging him not to have pity on the enemies. And they sang the praises of the GPU, "flaming sword of Soviet power." The dual objective of elim-inating the opponent and acquiring a consensus for repression was achieved. "The exacerbation of the class struggle within socialism" could no longer be stopped, nor did it have geographic boundaries.

We must be constantly on guard. . . .

Luigi Calligaris was a Communist from Trieste who had begun the struggle alongside Vidali. Arrested in 1926 for antifascist activities, he was imprisoned on the small islands of Favignana, Ustica, and finally Ponza. He managed to escape into exile, taking refuge in France, and from there he went to the Soviet Union. After working in a workshop in Kharkov, he requested permission to return to Italy several times in order to fight against fascism. But when the Comintern turned him down once again, he moved to Moscow, where he found work at the Kaganovich ball-bearing factory. There he distinguished himself so much for his work that he was praised and rewarded by management. But his friend-ship with Amadeo Bordiga, one of the founders of the Italian Communist Party, would prove fatal for him.

With three other Bordiga supporters, he created an opposition group in the heart of the Club of Emigrants, and he shared his negative opin-ions of Stalin with Vidali. Vidali was his compatriot and comrade during this time, although he would later publicly accuse him of leftist deviationism. After Kirov's assassination, Calligaris was arrested and sent to a gulag in the region of Archangel, where he contracted tuberculosis. All traces of him disappeared in 1936.

While she was living in Moscow, Modotti immersed herself once again in her political work. The only contact she had with the artistic and "cultural" environments was when she had to collect signatures for the endless petitions against "imperialist repression." Early on she again saw Sergei Eisenstein, who was working feverishly on the interminable editing of *Que viva México.* Jay Leyda, the U.S. film historian, contacted him when he went to Moscow in 1933, trying to locate Modotti. He delivered to her a package of photos that Alma Reed had kept for her, along with the book on Orozco's murals. Leyda was left with the impression of Modotti as a determined woman with very little free time due to the enormous amount of work she had to produce, and who was apparently satisfied with the security that she had finally achieved.

Lotte Jacobi also traveled to Moscow and went to visit Modotti in her room at the Soyuznaya Hotel. She asked her how she could no longer feel the need to take photographs, especially considering that all around the world there were magazines willing to buy pictures of the Soviet Union. Modotti responded dryly, "I cannot use the camera when there is still so much work to be done."

Maxim Gorky also visited from time to time, increasingly less enthusiastic about signing the declarations and appeals. The somber gray cloak that oppressed Muscovites also extended to the intellectual environment. Writers and poets ran the risk of deportation in the same way that, or perhaps more than, professional politicians did: The Party machine demanded exalted images that would serve as an inspiration to the public. Any doubt was regarded as defeatism.

Leopold Averbach was the secretary general of the Association of Proletarian Writers. A young parvenu particularly well qualified for a bureaucratic career, Averbach was the guardian of the Bolshevik ethic of poets and novelists. But after *Literature and Revolution* by Viktor Serge appeared in a Parisian publication, Averbach was removed from his position and his association was dissolved, accused of ineffectiveness for not having neutralized the dangerous author in time. Being the nephew of Yagoda, the head of Stalin's secret service from 1934 to 1936, he managed to save himself by making an absurd public condemnation of his "own cultural politics." When his protector fell, he too would be shot to death in 1937.

Sergei Yesenin, regarded as the greatest lyrical poet in Russia, locked himself in his hotel room and slit his wrist. He wrote his last verses in blood: "To die is not new in this life, but now it is not new either to live." Then he hanged himself with his belt from the boiler pipes. He had embraced the Revolution enthusiastically, and he had lived it with a passion that made him even more vulnerable to disillusion; he distanced himself from it only briefly in order to follow Isadora Duncan on her ceaseless travels across Europe, and he had married her with the same haste with which he did everything. When he returned to Moscow in 1922, he did not find any affinity with the new Soviet reality. Intolerant and secluded, he wrote: "There you have the relentless severity that sums up all the suffering of men! In the same way that the sickle cuts down the heavy ears of corn, the swan's neck is cut off. . . . I have been cruel, I have been fierce, but only to burn with greater fervor. . . . Today I am a foreigner in my own land."

A short while later the novelist Andrei Sobol, whose expressionism displeased the Party, took his own life. Once deported to Siberia by the czar, he fled into exile and returned to fight in the Caucasus against the White Army. In his last years he had been censured and marginalized.

Mayakovsky shot himself, as did Evgenya Bogdanovna Bos the day after the university purges. Litvinov killed himself, Glazman killed himself, the young Viktor Dimitriev and his wife killed themselves together, and the list became so extensive that the Central Committee of Control called a special session. The sharpest wits, the most sensitive hearts, and the innovative minds of the Soviet Union vanished inside the four walls of a hotel, behind desks buried in useless papers, destroyed by the same guns that had been used in the streets to shoot czarist officers and White Guards.

Whoever did not get out of the way and gathered the strength to cry out against the emptiness and the suffocation was persecuted relentlessly. Sometimes in a subtle and roundabout way, isolating them and preventing publication, more often in an abrupt way, as in the case of Pilnyak, an extremist writer in formalist antinarrative technique, who disappeared into thin air. Only after many years would it be discovered that he had died in a concentration camp. Ivanov Razumnik met the same fate; he was permitted to write only about literary themes, having been criticized for his "creativity prone to defeatism."

Multiple forms of censorship deformed and sterilized books. The editor of publications consulted the Office of Letters, which reviewed all manuscripts. After passing through the first filter, the official critic issued the verdict: worthy of being acquired by libraries; mere tolerance; or removal from circulation. After many years of research carried out by the best-known intellectuals in Leningrad, the complete edition of the *Encyclopedic Dictionary* was ordered destroyed because some words were "tendentious." Artem Vesely was silenced because he titled his novel *Bloodthirsty Russia*; Zamyatin, who had already been persecuted by the czarist police in 1914 for the subversive novel *At the End of the World*, was finished once and for all, now guilty of having published the satirical *Us*, precursor of the work of Huxley and Orwell. Thanks to the intervention of Gorky, he managed to save himself but was forced into exile.

Individual persecution was not enough; in addition, after each one, the rite of collective abjuration had to be carried out. And so, in succession, the survivors publicly condemned their traitorous colleagues. When the press denounced Zamyatin and Pilnyak as counterrevolutionaries, the writers of the association endorsed any type of condemnation they were advised to without hesitation, only later to run and ask forgiveness in private. Boris Pasternak did it, as did Aleksey Tolstoy, Fedin, Ivanov, Gorky . . . Max Eastman coined the expression "writers in uniform." However, there were also attempts at collective protest, like the harsh 1929 communiqué against defamation and administrative threats. It got no response, and as the years passed the heads of all those who had signed would fall, one after another.

Gorky did not explain himself, but inside the parlors where alcohol was consumed he stated, "In other times the Russian writer only had to fear the police and the archbishop. The Communist official today acts as much one as the other: he always wants to stick his dirty paws into your soul."

The cultural section of the Central Committee even went so far as to establish the plot of dramas and comedies for every situation. Whoever submitted to these directives and was able to detect the trend and protector at the time was assured economic success. Afinogenov became very rich in a short time with his play *The Aristocrats,* which was performed even in the most out-of-the-way theaters in Soviet Eurasia and was translated by International Editions into several languages. It dealt with saboteurs, priests, bandits, pickpockets, and prostitutes, all rehabilitated by healthy forced labor in the camps in the forests of the north; in the end they strolled along happily in new clothes, in an idyllic environment, happy about their repentance.

In the meantime, no sooner did young talented poets like Pavel Vasilyev begin to recite verses in some private residence, than they ended up in the basements of the GPU. The writer Victor Serge recounted from exile:

> What I would not know how to express in words is the atmosphere of humiliating stupidity at certain gatherings of writers reduced to zealous obedience. One day, in a dark little room in Herzen's house, we were listening to a report from Averbach on the kolkhozian spirit. Lunacharski, motionless in desolate boredom, sent me every now and then some ironic little notes, but he said nothing other than some formal words, in terms perhaps slightly more intelligent than the reporter's. Ernst Toller, who had recently gotten out of a Bavarian prison, sat between the two of us. The entire discourse was translated for him word for word, and his big dark eyes, his face that expressed strength yet at the same time gentleness, had an expression of confused astonishment. In the confinement of a rebel poet, he had surely imagined Soviet literature in a very different way. And I remember a session of our writers' syndicate in Leningrad in which a few young writers, nearly illiterate, proposed forming search teams to go and remove from secondhand booksellers those works of history that the "Chief" had recently criticized. The room was embarrassingly silent.

Nineteen

Modotti joined Vidali in Belgium, where they worked together to reestablish a series of contacts, traveling to Bruges, Ghent, Ostende, and Antwerp. Later Vidali received orders to return to Moscow, and Modotti was sent to Paris. According to French Party beliefs, her Red Aid activities had still not been discovered by the security services. She remained there for five months, during which she coordinated the international support network for refugees and political prisoners.

When she returned to the Soviet Union, Modotti was once again completely absorbed in internal propaganda work. But it was increasingly difficult for her to speak in the factories and workshops about the achievements of the workers' movement. Those faces before her, that listened to the often incomprehensible reports of faraway officials, seemed to grow gloomier each day. Most people took refuge in a passive inertia, their only defense against the spiral of madness that led to a succession of "confessions" of treason and an uninterrupted pattern of executions. One after another, men who had been respected as fathers of the Revolution, and who had been admired for the self-denial and sacrifice with which they had built the immense Soviet Union, marched through court-rooms admitting that they deserved punishment. The inability to under-stand generated apathy and denial, and the distrust worked its way into even the closest relationships. It was not just the next-door neighbor who represented a potential informer, but the friend and comrade of so many battles: even the person with whom you shared your life could have been responsible for issuing weekly reports, in which your words were recorded, or the spontaneous venting or the curse that escaped because of yet one more outrage, or because of the growing shortage of food.

Modotti slowly slipped into a crisis of hopelessness, which manifested itself in silence and a sadness in all her actions. The only way to escape from that deathly atmosphere was to try to secure a new mission abroad. She even entertained the idea of secretly entering Italy again, but she did not dare speak openly about it: In order to avoid being accused of inter-fering in the internal affairs of another country, Moscow had never granted permits to Italians who wanted to return and fight fascism. All who had requested it automatically ended up on a list of suspects. The opportunity came up a few months later, when Vittorio Vidali was as-signed a mission in Spain.

In October 1934 a great workers' revolt had broken out in Asturias. It was led by the anarchists and concluded with the overthrowing of local power and the introduction of self-rule. But the central government, after having reorganized the army, launched a powerful counterattack that would be resolved after a twenty-day battle that left thousands dead and resulted in more than thirty thousand arrests. The merciless repres-sion and swift executions were not enough, however, to contain the now uncontrollable revolutionary drive. The government tried to restrain it by handing in its resignation and announcing new elections in February 1936. The Spanish situation was being watched from Moscow with growing apprehension. Anarchists and Trotskyites represented the large majority of the popular movement, and, without any hesitation, the Comintern decided to intervene. The ablest agents and officials were sent to Madrid, Barcelona, Valencia, and Zaragoza.

Only a few weeks after his return to Moscow, Vidali was informed of his transfer to Spain. Modotti shared with him her fears about the subtle surveillance under which she had been for some time. It seemed that un-

clear "rumors from abroad" were circulating about her supposed sympathies toward Trotskyism, and as a result all her work and private activities were being continuously watched. The idea that she had formed of
the Soviet Union during the first few months had now been destroyed by
the stifling climate that enveloped her life as an obscure official. Spain
represented an opportunity to get away from Moscow, and Modotti at
once submitted her request to go there. In November 1935, the Comintern informed her of its decision: She would spend a few days in Paris
and then travel on to Madrid.

Certain that she would never return to the Soviet Union, Tina said
good-bye to the few friends she had left. She spent her last night in
Moscow with Vidali, at the home of the Kornaciuks.

Ivan Kornaciuk had participated in the October Revolution as a member
of the Guard, later joining the Red Army in order to continue the war
against the White Armies. After the defeat of the last Cossack divisions,
Ivan devoted himself to the *besprisorniki*, the numerous vagabond children whom the civil war had left orphaned and abandoned in the streets.
Kornaciuk was thirty-eight years old, tall, thin, and slightly stooped, and
he had a gentle look behind his tiny glasses. He was married to Hava, a
teacher, a very beautiful woman who had aged prematurely. Modotti visited them often, in spite of the fact that their house was now under
constant police surveillance. Militants of the leftist opposition, the Kornaciuks had been thrown out of the Party in 1927 and later readmitted
after rigorous self-criticism, but their loyalty was now in question because of the new "exacerbation of the class struggle." That night, the
couple managed to maintain an atmosphere of affectionate happiness in
front of Modotti, but a sadness hung over their attempts to forget the reality outside and devote themselves to the friend who was preparing to
leave them. Vidali's presence did not help to calm the climate of palpable
anxiety in the house: They knew that he was firmly on the other side of
the abyss, but they did not display any suspicions in front of him, wel-
coming him only as a friend of Modotti. Hava's mother, however, could
not hide what she felt, and she said good-bye to her with a desperate hug
and a terrified look.

During dinner they spoke about the October Revolution, later moving on to recent political changes in Europe, the situation in France, the German drama, and the isolation of the antifascists in Italy. Not a single word was spoken about the Soviet Union.

Before saying good-bye forever, Kornaciuk found an excuse to take Modotti aside. He told her that they had been under constant surveillance for at least eight years. Abandoning the pretense of forced cordiality, he expressed all his bitterness and his resignation to his imminent end. While they had allowed him to work and survive with some dignity for the last few years, the recommencement of the purges after Kirov's murder had implicated him so that there was no chance of escape. During the many trials and resulting executions, Kornaciuk was interrogated several times and finally expelled with his companion. Immediately thereafter they both lost their jobs. Now he was just waiting to be arrested. But he no longer feared for his own life; his tone was now of someone resigned to an inevitable fate, with no strength to react or motivation to resist. Instead he was terrified about what would happen to his children. After parents were arrested, the rule demanded that the children be "degraded" in front of all students: their red pioneer handkerchiefs and their *komsomol* card would be taken from them, because they would be considered "enemies of the nation." After having taken care of the *besprisorniki* for years, Ivan Kornaciuk could not even imagine that the fate of his own offspring would be to end up in a collection center for abandoned children.

Modotti did not open her mouth the entire way back to the hotel with Vidali. She stopped at the door and glanced at the black, moonless sky, at the ice that covered the dark streets with a uniform varnish, and at the bare, skeletal trees. After a long sigh, she spoke the few words that summarized her feelings on her life in Moscow:

"I am happy to be leaving."

Twenty

E ven today in discussions about the civil war and the Francoist coup,
Spain is described as having been abandoned by the European
democracies and helped only by the Soviet Union, which could not resist
the impact of German and Italian military intervention. In fact, Stalin
did the exact opposite of what his heirs would later have us believe. He
did intervene with military cadres and weapons, but only to prevent a
hypothetical revolution in Spain. According to his logic, it was under-
standable: The Spanish masses had organized independently of the tiny
Communist Party, aligning themselves toward libertarian ideologies and
practices, in keeping with their antistate, anticlerical roots, which had
their origin in a social reality completely different from that of the Soviet
Union.

   The syndicate with the most supporters was the anarchist Confederación Nacional del Trabajo, while the Federación Anarquista Ibérica
had another two million members and controlled all of Catalonia, the region that historically drove the country. The most important industries
sprang up there, and they relied on an active proletariat that took re-

sponsibility for the self-management of the mechanical and textile factories. In the countryside it had been several years since the viability of agricultural communes had been demonstrated, expropriating land from large landowners and organizing production and distribution by representation. Most Spanish Marxists did not identify with Moscow's directives either, creating the Partido Obrero de Unidad Marxista (POUM), whose inspiration was not directly Trotskyite but decidedly anti-Stalinist.

With the Popular Front's victory in the elections of February 16, 1935, the families that unlawfully held economic power, joined by church leaders, pushed the military ranks to revolt. The outbreak of hostilities also represented the long-awaited chance for all-out intervention by the Comintern in a situation that, more than any other, was impairing the principle of "revolution in a single country." And a civil war was the most suitable climate for identifying and attacking the leading figures of the opposition, as well as favoring manipulations of all kinds.

In the framework of the complicated and very fragile international balance of power, there were even those who maintained that Vyackeslev Molotov was already plotting the pact with Joachim von Ribbentrop and the alliance with Nazi Germany and that reciprocal neutrality in "de facto" battles had been ratified. This was a policy that the Soviet Union would respect in Spain, if not in appearance, at least in the goals and results. The political commissioners' unyielding control of the International Brigades immediately led to brutal eliminations and summary executions in the ranks of dissidents, finding complete support from the Republican government, whose efforts were intended more to dismantle the popular militias than to fight rebel officials. "First war, then revolution" would be the demagogic slogan aimed at conquering the base of the UGT, the Socialist-Communist-inspired syndicate. But in practice Stalin would furnish those few warlike means only to guarantee the legitimacy of his agents' actions. The principal task was to prevent Trotskyite theories about "permanent revolution" from being introduced and extended to other countries, and to consolidate the image of the Soviet Union as the only point of reference for all Communist parties around the world. Such an objective could be endangered by the Spanish revolution, already under way and in clear opposition to Moscow.

Vittorio Vidali's operative title was that of political commissioner of the Fifth Regiment, the military formation responsible for administering Stalinist objectives from within the Republican army. Vidali was a man of action, impulsive, courageous, and "creative" in tactical work, endowed with great charisma and an innate charm. Impetuous, always inclined toward anticonformist behavior, he was preceded by a reputation in which the pistol and amorous conquests were united; before reaching the age of forty he was already a bit of a legend. But he did not possess sufficient political strength or sufficient strategic foresight to be able to carry out subtle plans without resorting to blatant interventions, a factor that would often force the leaders of the Comintern to stop his actions. Therefore, he had to report the strict execution of orders to Togliatti, who, cognizant of the serious responsibilities and accusations to which he had to respond, would go so far as denying his physical presence in Spain. Holding the post of proconsul from July 1937 until the final days of the republic, Togliatti managed to erase from official history the many crimes perpetrated by the Comintern agents under his direct orders. And those who were spared would continue to denounce them uselessly due to their precarious situation as exiles and heretics; at the same time, turning toward a Europe devastated by war, they saw in Stalin their only hope of weakening the Wehrmacht. In any case, many of those voices would be silenced by the precise and detailed work of a dense network of hired assassins as skillful as they were merciless. And a few scandalous cases would demonstrate an obtuse absence of political opportunism tied to a considerable dose of vindictive paranoia. The first would be the assassination of Trotsky.

The disappearance of many lesser-known figures would provoke much less clamor. If in Russia executions were taking place at a constant pace and without "image problems," in other countries the elimination of political adversaries was frequently characterized by the concealment of the real causes and even of the methods used. In this way an impressive number of strange accidents, disappearances, suicides, and "heart attacks" would be hastily filed away.

Vidali arrived in Madrid on July 18, 1936, the day after the revolt of French legionnaires and Moroccan troops. That same day he called the delegates of Red Aid together in order to give them instructions, and then he moved on to the barracks on Francos Rodríguez Street, where he would organize the formation of the Fifth Regiment.

Modotti joined him on July 19, and she was sent to the Hospital Obrero, where volunteers were urgently needed, as fascist doctors and religious nurses had fled. The reorganization of the wards and operating rooms was just beginning when the first trucks full of wounded began to descend upon them. Very soon the hospital would be transformed into an infernal tornado: Bandages and medicine ran out in a few days, amputations had to be performed without anesthesia, and many volunteer nurses died, poisoned by the cyanide that a Falangist (a member of the Spanish fascist organization Falange) had slipped into the food. Tina took charge of keeping watch on the kitchens, sleeping in a chair with her gun resting on her knees.

Later Modotti met the Canadian doctor Norman Bethune, and she offered to help him with his project of performing transfusions in the countryside and in the nearby rear guard, as most of the wounded bled to death before reaching the hospital. Tina also enlisted in the female battalion of the Fifth, where they taught her to use light weapons and to launch grenades. It was customary to adopt a war name, and she chose "María," after the Mexican custom of giving the name María to abandoned girls and young street vagrants.

But Modotti, although far from Moscow and its harsh climate, had not come to Spain as just any volunteer. She was a close collaborator of the political commissioner "Carlos Contreras," and although she tried to stay out of the way of the maneuvers of the Stalinist agents with whom she was forced to live, the Comintern considered her experience as an official to be more valuable than her current work as a nurse. Therefore they sent her to work in the propaganda section, and she began to distribute material in the rear guard, to participate in meetings, and to support without any enthusiasm the heroic effort of the Soviet nation and the brilliant example of its leaders.

In the meantime the Fifth Regiment was becoming the military-political mechanism entrusted with controlling the Republican army from within. However, the extremely strict order and rigid discipline were just a front: The fate of the Fifth would not be to fight the Falangists but rather to eliminate any form of "deviationism." In a short time the Communist nucleus of militias expanded and came to include thousands of men, until it assumed the proportions of a division structured in brigades and companies. Weapons and logistical support were not lacking: The supplies sent by Stalin served only to reinforce the prestige and influence of the Fifth Regiment, which would be used to dismantle agricultural communes and to disarm volunteers not incorporated into the army. The fusion of the Fifth with the armed forces was decided when Moscow's control had already spread to the Republican government, shortly before Togliatti's arrival.

In the first few months of the war, the advance of the legionnaires was almost completely blocked by the International Brigades and by the anarchist columns, while the government lost a few precious days vacillating over whether or not to distribute weapons to the volunteers. The rapid mobilization of antifascists from many different countries was also due to the popular Olympics in Barcelona, which had been arranged as an alternative to those taking place in Nazi Germany and which had attracted to Spain thousands of militants from the international Left. On the Aragon front, a squadron formed by the Englishman Tom Man, the German Ernst Thaelmann, who headed a battalion of an international brigade made up of German and Austrian volunteers, and the Italian Carlo Rosselli rushed to block the Falangist offensive. Founder of the Justice and Liberty Movement, Rosselli had in vain called a meeting in Paris in order to urge intervention on the side of the Spanish libertarians. But the Communists and Socialists, joined by the unity of action pact, had refused to interfere in "internal matters" of another nation, according to the policy maintained by the Comintern. Three days after the attack on Franco, Justice and Liberty decided to fight without any support, relying only on the anarchists and minority groups of the revolutionary Left.

Other Italian volunteers joined the French and the Poles in Gastone Sozzi's squadrons, called the Commune of Paris and Dombrovsky, concentrated in Irún, while the Hungarians formed the Rakosi group. The Americans assembled in the Lincoln Brigade and the Canadians in the Mackenzie-Papinau Regiment. But men and women from many different countries were found in many formations, to such an extent that in the

Dimitrov Battalion alone twelve languages were spoken. Thousands had come down from the Scandinavian countries, and, although fewer in number, contingents also arrived from India, China, South Africa, Abyssinia, Mexico, and Algeria.

The Republican army delayed the beginning of the counteroffensive. Before doing anything, it had to appease the most militant factions within headquarters. The Communists, on the other hand, devoted themselves exclusively to trying to infiltrate the military and political ranks and to carefully controlling the volunteers who crossed the border: the order was to identify the better-known figures of the Stalinist opposition.

In November, after their advance from Talavera and Maqueda and the fall of Toledo, Francoists were knocking on the doors of Madrid. The government fled hastily to Valencia in a disorganized flight that the residents of the capital did not hesitate to label as a betrayal. The Communists took advantage of the void in power and named one of their loyalists, Antonios Mije, as head of the defense. But it was the people of Madrid who drove back the first Falange attacks, positioning themselves spontaneously on the perimeter of the city. A few days later the International Brigades rushed in from the less involved fronts. The Durruti column came down from Aragón and took up positions in the university area. With some poorly maintained planes, André Malraux formed the Lafayette shooting squadron, with which he tried to oppose the Stukas of the German Condor Legion and the Savoia Marchettis of the Italian air force. The Francoist air force was equipped almost entirely with Fiats and Capronis, regarded at the time as some of the most advanced machines in European armies.

The climate of euphoric brotherhood of the first few days had now become one of divisions and internal conflicts that would soon end in bloody revenge. The first suspicious death was that of Buenaventura Durruti, the popular anarchist commander. His column was a rare example of efficiency and self-discipline. Equipped with its own health services and field kitchen, it also had a printing press, set up on trucks, which published a weekly, *Frente*, as well as millions of pamphlets and posters. News on the developments in the war and political commentaries were spread throughout Europe from its powerful radio station, which contributed to a rush of new volunteers.

For the international anarchist movement, the "iron column" was now a legend. Durruti's reputation could not be sullied, not even by the Communists. Only in the Soviet Union, thanks to Ilya Ehrenburg's reports, was he a target of all kinds of lies and tricks. When Zaragoza fell to the Falangists and was occupied by the fanatical "Requetés" (Carlist volunteers), of Navarra, who transformed it into a cemetery, the Durruti column was the only one to advance, camping twenty kilometers outside the city. But the government sent no help, preferring to lose the vitally important strategic point rather than encourage the popularity of the anarchists.

When Madrid, too, was about to fall, Durruti decided to come to its defense with five thousand men from the column. On November 13 the entire city cheered as he passed, shouting "Long live Madrid without government!" After a week of brutal combat, the legionnaires and the Moroccan troops were stopped along a line that went from the Plaza de la Moncloa to the Parque del Oeste. On November 19 Durruti inspected the front during a lull to assure that there were no weak points in the defensive formation of the troops. He was hit in the zone not exposed to enemy fire.

Durruti's funeral turned into a vast public demonstration in which hundreds of thousands of people and delegates from all political groups participated. The Communists also paid homage to him, supporting the official version of a stray bullet, but at the same time spreading the rumor that anarchists rebelling against military discipline had killed him. Vidali did not miss the chance to state that Durruti had shot himself as he got out of the car, with the barrel of the machine gun turned absurdly toward his chest, as if he had been using the weapon as a walking stick. The men in the column avoided openly accusing the Communists in order to avert a bloody uproar at a time when the front ran the risk of collapsing, and they affirmed that a man from the Republican Civil Guard was the one who had shot from the window of an abandoned building. Some years later the French Communist leader Auguste Lecoeur would calmly admit, "We were the ones who made him disappear." (It should be pointed out that in the days following Durruti's death, all the best-known figures of anarchism in Madrid took refuge in Catalonia, the stronghold of the libertarian movement.)

The many vicissitudes of the civil war, condemned to a slow defeat by massive foreign intervention but damaged above all by internal conspiracies, contributed to a large number of unexplained deaths and disappearances. The majority of the anti-Stalinists killed by "stray bullets" or dragged to secret torture chambers by the GPU would appear among the nameless fallen or those "missing in action." But the accusations of fighters who had survived would rise through some of the better-known figures of the leftist opposition, who fought for decades to not forget the new world order.

After having organized the armed resistance to the Black Shirts during his days in Parma, Guido Picelli had taken refuge in Moscow, where he earned the rank of Instructor Captain of the Red Army. In late 1936 he was in Paris. There he was introduced by the secretary of the Italian Extremist Socialist Party to Julián Gorkin, a member of the executive committee of the POUM. "I am not a Communist," he clarified immediately. "I left the Soviet Union because I want to use my experience to serve the international and Spanish antifascist cause. But I have nothing to do with the Communists. If I can be of use to you, I am offering to organize an assault battalion."

Gorkin furnished Picelli with the means to go to Barcelona, scheduling a meeting a few days later. They met in the Catalonian capital at a session of the executive committee. Picelli was sent to the front with the rank of captain, leaving two hours after his assistant, José Rovira, the commander of the military wing of the POUM. When he was about to get in his car near the Hotel Colón, headquarters of the central committee of the Partido Socialista Unificado de Cataluña (PSUC), a stranger approached and asked him to follow him in order to clear up a matter quickly. Guido Picelli, not suspecting a trap, let himself be led away. About a month later, newspapers reported that the "Italian captain Guido Picelli has fallen fighting heroically on the Madrid front."

Subsequent investigations of Gorkin revealed that the encounter in Paris had taken place in the office occupied by the government of the

"Generalitat," led by a former associate of Andrés Nin in the Justice Council, León Dalty. But the GPU had succeeded in placing a telephone operator and a secretary there; thus, they had learned of Picelli's decision and then followed him, waiting for the most favorable moment.

Unlike Hans Beimler, the former German Communist delegate who was murdered and buried in Madrid, Guido Picelli received an impressive funeral: The mob, surrounded by visibly armed squads of soldiers and police, was made to parade past the headquarters of the POUM and the PSUC. It was a clear warning to Trotskyites and to that minority of social-ist revolutionaries who had not supported the pact with the Communists.

The English Marxist Friend, suspected of sympathizing with the Trot-skyites, was taken to a Soviet boat on the pretext of using his expertise as a radio technician to repair damage on board. Transferred to Odessa, on April 12 he entered a GPU prison. From that day forward all traces of him were lost. The son of Labour Party member Smillie was murdered in a Spanish jail controlled by political commissioners of the Comintern; in the meantime, the son of Russian Socialist leader R. Abramovich, Mark Rien, also disappeared.

Modotti's primary activity was to organize and coordinate the work of Red Aid. But what at first had been an international solidarity network for the victims of repression from all dictatorships had now become an instrument of Stalinist counterespionage. W. G. Krivitsky, the high offi-cial of the intelligence service of the General Staff of the Red Army, would write a memorandum that contained explicit references to the So-viet intervention in Spain. And he maintained that since June 30, 1934, Stalin had begun negotiations for an alliance with Hitler, a decision reached during a meeting of the Politburo in which Krivitsky himself had participated.

> In Europe we have created a certain number of secret control points, where each aspiring volunteer must be subjected to a new and detailed investigation by foreign Communists, loyal and worthy of absolute trust, or secretaries and agents of organizations under our control, like Interna-tional Red Aid, Friends of Republican Spain . . . or of officials of several Spanish institutions tied to us. As the former Ambassador of Republican

Spain in France, Luis de Araquistáin, has demonstrated, ninety percent of all the important posts in the Ministry of War were most recently filled by men loyal to Stalin. The GPU's control over those volunteers considered worthy of sacrificing their lives for what they believed to be the cause of the Republic also continues in Spain, where informers are living with the troops in order to either discover possible spies, eliminate all who display opposing political convictions or keep an eye on the readings and conversations of the volunteers. In practice, all the political commissioners of the International Brigades, just as later also most of the commissioners of the Republican Army, are members of the Party. Passports are taken from the volunteers when they arrive in Spain, and they are rarely returned. And in the case of a discharge, the document is declared lost. Passports of the fallen, after several weeks of investigating the family members, are easily adapted to GPU agents for new missions.

And it was with one of these passports that "María," like Vidali, was sent to the United States after the Spanish defeat. The hired assassin whom Stalin sent to Mexico to assassinate Leon Trotsky also used the document of a murdered volunteer.

Regarding the situation in Catalonia, Krivitsky wrote:

Sslutski, the head of the foreign affairs section of the GPU, received an order from Moscow to inspect the secret police, organized after the Soviet model. The GPU now controls almost all the territory in Republican Spain, but it is concentrating its action in Catalonia, where independent groups are stronger and also the Trotskyites show a certain presence. Upon his return to Paris a few weeks later, Sslutski said to me, "They have good material down there, but they lack experience. We cannot allow Spain to become an open battle field for anti-Soviet elements who have come here from around the world. When all is said and done, we must consider that 'our' Spain already forms part of the Soviet front. We must make it strong for ourselves. Who knows how many spies there may be among the volunteers. The anarchists and Trotskyites are also our enemies, although they must be considered as anti-Fascist militants. Therefore, they must be eliminated." And the GPU is working brilliantly. In December 1936, terror already reigned in Madrid, Barcelona and Valencia. The GPU has its special prisons, and its men are carrying out the ordered assassinations and abductions.

Twenty-One

B arcelona, the capital of Catalonia, was the birthplace of all the antiauthoritarian ideologies in the Iberian Peninsula. Anarchist militiamen controlled the entire region, helped by the Marxists of the POUM in the social and economic administration of the city. In order to support the Communist slogan "First war, then revolution," and to create a common cause against Franco, four anarchists entered the government as ministers, the first and only case in history.

The consolidation of the FAI-CNT was due not just to the collectivization of factories and farms, but also to the rapid armed reaction to the rebellion: Columns of armed workers and the people of Barcelona themselves had defeated troops chosen and commanded by generals considered to be among the best in the Spanish army. But after almost a year of war, the city was the stage for reciprocal attacks between Communists and anarchists, in a blow-for-blow vendetta that saw many CNT leaders murdered on their doorsteps; for each CNT death, the body of an official of the General Workers Union (UGT) was found in the street a short time later. The responsibilities of the "fifth column" were limited, as it comprised only a small number of individuals who lacked concrete plans and directives. Actually it was the network of Stalinist agents who, from the rear guard, drove this civil war within a civil war, while the government pressed for the disarmament of the militias and not a single gun arrived in Barcelona from Moscow. Shipments of weapons and ammunition were an exclusive privilege of those sections that were under the control of the political commissioners of the Comintern. These well-equipped troops would have been able to drive back the Falangists in Zaragoza and force them back to the Atlantic Coast. But the orders were to let the Durruti column bleed and to remain in Catalonia and await developments. In this respect the article that appeared in *Pravda* on December 17, 1936, was enlightening: "A purge of Trotskyite and anarchists elements has begun in Catalonia, and it will be carried out with the same energy as in the Soviet Union."

The pretext for beginning the *final solution* was conceived on May 3, 1937, when the Communists accused the anarchists of interfering with and boycotting the telephone communications of the president. The telephone exchange, like most services in Barcelona, was self-managed by employees and workers affiliated with the FAI-CNT.

George Orwell, a volunteer in the International Brigades and a POUM sympathizer, was one of the eyewitnesses. Around midday he left his hotel and ran into a friend who told him, "Something is going on at the telephone exchange." At first Orwell paid no attention, but in the afternoon, as he was crossing the Ramblas, he heard several gunshots in the distance. Immediately afterward, a group of young anarchists with red-and-black handkerchiefs around their necks and rifles in hand, took up positions on the corners of some of the side streets. An American doctor who had been on the front with Orwell stopped suddenly in front of him and took him by the arm, extremely nervous. Excited, he managed to explain that in the Plaza de Cataluña a large number of trucks filled with Civil Guards had surrounded the telephone exchange and then attacked it. Then came the unexpected arrival of armed anarchists, who immediately counterattacked.

As Orwell and the doctor were heading for the plaza, a truck sped by them at full speed, filled with guns and anarchist flags. The image that remained engraved in the English writer's mind was that of a disheveled young boy in rags, lying facedown on the roof covered with mattresses, clutching a machine gun. Orwell had the feeling that, at least in the early hours, nobody really understood what was going on. The only thing that was certain was that the Civil Guard had attacked the anarchist workers at the telephone exchange. "The issue was clear enough," Orwell would write in *Homage to Catalonia.* "On the one side the CNT, on the other side the police. I have no particular love for the idealized 'worker' as he appears in the bourgeois Communist's mind, but when I see an actual flesh-and-blood worker in conflict with his natural enemy, the policeman, I do not have to ask myself which side I am on."

The brutal work of the Civil Guard, whose loyalty to antifascism was in question, could only provoke bloody incidents. With the fuse lit, all it could do was stop the imminent fire from spreading. The battalion of the Forty-sixth Division, made up almost entirely of anarchist fighters, and those of the Twenty-ninth, in which those of the POUM were incorporated, converged on Barcelona to drive back the Communist coup. But the military command managed to falsify the news, assuring the respective commanders that it was merely a police provocation that had already been resolved. Therefore the front should not be left unprotected because of a slight problem of public order. The two divisions stopped their advance and returned to the front lines. At that time the central government sent five thousand assault guards, a corps of militiamen of unquestionable Communist loyalty, who disembarked in the port and, after violent combat, occupied the strategic points in the city.

Official figures would report four hundred dead and one thousand wounded. The hunt for heretics was on. Following Stalin's maniacal aversion toward everything that smelled of Trotskyism, the principal target was the POUM. Not being able to count on a wide popular base like the FAI-CNT, the POUM was accused of betraying the Republican cause, and they were falsely accused of making agreements with the Francoists. Leaders and militants were hunted down, arrested, and prosecuted.

George Orwell's name appeared at the top of the list of the GPU. He escaped capture by chance, not returning to the hotel where his wife was waiting for him. Alone she endured the inrush of the police and Stalinist officials:

The police conducted the search in the recognized GPU or Gestapo style. In the small hours of the morning there was a pounding on the door, and six men marched in, switched on the light and immediately took up various positions about the room, obviously agreed upon beforehand. They then searched both rooms (there was a bathroom attached) with inconceivable thoroughness. They sounded the walls, took up the mats, examined the floor, felt the curtains, probed under the bath and the radiator, emptied every drawer and suitcase and felt every garment and held it up to the light. They impounded all papers, including the contents of the waste-paper basket, and all our books into the bargain. They were thrown into ecstasies of suspicion by finding that we possessed a French translation of Hitler's *Mein Kampf.* If that had been the only book they found our doom would have been sealed. It is obvious that a person who reads *Mein Kampf* must be a Fascist. The next moment, however, they came upon a copy of Stalin's pamphlet, *Ways of Liquidating Trotskyists and Other Double Dealers*, which reassured them somewhat. . . .

That night McNair, Cottman, and I slept in some long grass at the edge of a derelict building-lot.

After five days in hiding, Orwell reached the border and took refuge in France.

Many others did not have time to escape or to defend themselves. On May 5, Camillo Berneri, the anarchist from Lodi who had been one of the organizers of the first Italian column, was captured by a group of armed men. The following morning his body was found lying on a Barcelona street. After having fought on the front, Berneri edited an Italian newspaper, *Guerra di classe,* and he was writing a book entitled *Mussolini alla conquista delle Baleari* (Mussolini: Conquest of the Balearics), in which he intended to reveal the sending of Soviet aid to fascist Italy, in support of the campaign in Ethiopia. Until then the collaboration among the Comintern, Hitler, and Mussolini, something the anarchists were certain was taking place, could not be irrefutably proven. This may explain in part why Berneri was murdered. A close friend of his, Umberto Tommasini of Trieste, who distinguished himself in the war as a fighter behind enemy lines, accused Vittorio Vidali of the murder. However, the Communists' posture with respect to Berneri's elimination was not very clear. When historian Gaetano Salvemini accused the Communists of being behind the murder, Togliatti branded the accusations "anti-Communist lies." These claims were proved baseless in Giuseppe di Vittorio's vindication of Berneri in *La Voce degli italiani.*

Those who knew Modotti at that time remembered her as being exhausted, indifferent, and protected by an armor of insensitivity. One morning she was expressionless, watching a chase that resulted in civilians being shot down in the streets. Standing motionless, she did not express the slightest emotion at that pile of dismembered flesh, at the cries of the children who clung to their mothers.

The few times she exchanged words with someone, she spoke of "collective madness," of monstrous mechanisms that had already gotten out of hand, and she was amazed at her own indifference toward death.

An increasing number of "specialists" entrusted with taking command of the army and of the police arrived from Moscow. The government, blackmailed by the promise of aid, limited itself to ratifying with euphemistic decisions what was in fact an actual passage of power.

Gen. Enrique Lister, who formed part of the diminished circle of friends whom Vidali and Modotti still saw regularly, took charge of dissolving the agricultural communes, returning the land to the large landowners, and ordering sections of the army to intervene in the self-managed factories. Military ranks were also reintroduced, along with the obligatory salute to superiors and the principle of hierarchy. A decree imposed the extinction of popular self-defense, prohibiting anyone not wearing a government uniform from carrying a weapon.

In June, Andrés Nin, the founder of the POUM, was abducted. His international reputation put Republicans in serious trouble, as they did not know how to respond to the avalanche of protests that rose up in Spain and abroad. Jesús Hernández, a Communist official who in a book would later denounce crimes in which he had also been an accomplice, described the conclusion of the "Nin case" as follows:

> Andrés Nin, who had been a friend of Lenin, Kamenev, Zinoviev and Trotsky, was assassinated in Spain in the same way his comrades from the old Bolshevik guard were assassinated in the Soviet Union.

Orlov, head of the GPU in Spain, ordered his abduction in order to force a confession out of him in which he was to acknowledge that he was a spy in the service of Franco. . . . Nin's torture began with the "dry" method: a relentless persecution lasting ten, twenty, thirty hours during which the torturers take turns repeating the same questions: "Confess, declare, admit. . . ." It is a scientific method that tends to destroy the individual's mental energy, to demoralize him.

But Andrés Nin's resistance was incredible. There was no trace of physical or moral decline in him; no sign of that mental division that pushed old associates of Lenin to the unprecedented abdication of all willpower, to the conviction that seemed transplanted in their moribund brain: Stalin is killing me, but Stalin is not the revolution or the Party either. And now that my death is inevitable, I will make a final sacrifice for my people and my ideal, and declare myself to be a counterrevolutionary and a criminal, so that the homeland can survive.

Nin, on the other hand, did not give in. His torturers lost control. They decided to abandon the dry method, and they began to pull off his skin, to tear the muscles, and to make his suffering reach the limit of human resistance. Nevertheless, Andrés Nin endured even the most "refined" tortures. After a few days his face had become a shapeless mass of swollen flesh. Orlov seemed frantic, driven mad by the fear of scandal, exasperated before this dying man who, nevertheless, refused to denounce his comrades.

Life was fading away in him. All of loyalist Spain and the entire world were shaken by the campaign for his freedom; they demanded to know the truth: where he was and who had taken him prisoner. But to let him go alive would have meant a double scandal: the proof of the horrible torture inflicted and the denunciation of Stalin's behavior in Spain. They decided to eliminate him, and they discussed what method to use. Bury him? Burn him? But the responsibility for his abduction had already fallen on the GPU, and they had to think of a way to free the Communists from the weight of this disappearance and at the same time show that Nin was guilty of collaborating with the enemy.

The solution came from the most demonic of Orlov's associates, Commandant Carlos, Vittorio Vidali, as he was called in Italy, or Carlos T. Contreras, the name he had used in Mexico and now in Spain. His plan was the following: simulate an abduction by false agents of the Gestapo disguised as volunteers of the International Brigades, who would attack the prison in Alcalá and make Nin disappear once and for all. Then the rumor would be spread that he had been "liberated" by the Nazis, further evidence of their contacts with national and international Fascism. As for the body, Vidali proposed to simply throw it into the sea after weighting it down. For Orlov, the trick seemed a bit crude, but there was no other way out.

So, one day the two men who were watching over the prisoner in the penitentiary in Alcalá de Henares were found tied and gagged. Two Communists affiliated with the Socialist Party stated that they had been attacked by a group of at least ten militiamen from the International Brigades. They had opened the prisoner's cell and taken him away by car. To lend more credibility to the leftist staging, they had "forgotten" Nin's bag full of documents with seals and letterhead that proved his relationship with the German espionage service.

The day after Andrés Nin's death, comrade X informed me of having transmitted the following message to Moscow: "A.N. matter settled with procedure A." According to the code of the Soviet delegation, "procedure A" indicated elimination. If Nin had not been eliminated, the delegation, made up of Togliatti, Codovilla, Stepanov and Gheroe, would have sent a message without mentioning "matter settled."

On June 25, 1937, the organ of the Spanish Communist Party, *Mundo Obrero*, published an article entitled "The Escape of the Outlaw Nin," in which it maintained that the Falangists were the perpetrators of the attack on the prison in Alcalá, and that Andrés Nin was possibly now in Burgos under Franco's protection.

Twenty-Two

In the spring of 1937, Modotti was transferred to Valencia. She had just received news of the death of her mother, who had left the United States in 1930 to return with Mercedes to Trieste, where her daughter Valentina was living. It was Mercedes who wrote to her, using a Paris address, and a Red Aid militant saw that she received the correspondence. Many of these letters were intercepted by the OVRA, and the copies would remain in the archives at police headquarters in Trieste. Among these was a reply from Modotti to Mercedes.

The letter in which you talk about the death of our dear mother did not reach me until last week. I never received the previous ones, in which I imagine you spoke of her illness. Thank you for the delicate way that you gave me the news, as it has helped me to bear the pain. But I wasn't able to write to you immediately. My only wish at that time was to be near my brothers and sisters, because our closeness, yours especially, would have made the suffering less terrible and filled a bit of the enormous and terrible void I feel. . . . I have to make an effort to hold back tears as I am

*writing to you. I have to be strong. I know that if circumstances had been
different, I would have been able to see my mother again in these last ten
years. It's a thought that makes me deeply angry about everything that
prevented me from doing so.*

In Valencia, Modotti took part in the Second International Congress
for the Defense of Culture against Fascism, where she met Ernest Hemingway and Malraux. She again saw Pablo Neruda, Cabada, and
Siqueiros who, after having held the post of military attaché in the Mexican Embassy in Paris, had come to Spain to enlist in General Lister's
Eleventh Division. But like the other political commissioners, Siqueiros
did not fight against the Francoists on the front: His war experience was
regarded as secondary to that as Party leader. The installation of the Republican government in Valencia brought about the concentration of the
Comintern's most loyal men. For Moscow, the die had already been cast.

From the window of Modotti's top-floor room, the mouth of the
Guadalaviar could be seen, and among the tangle of shipyards and
cranes were tiny gray islands, piles of sandbags that from far away
looked like termites' nests that had sprung up absurdly among the port
installations. They were the antiaircraft batteries, cannon, and machine
guns that howled helplessly at the sky, trying to drive back the clouds of
bombers that took off nonstop from the Balearics. After Madrid the long
torment had also begun for Valencia. She drew the curtains, sat down at
the table, and again began to look through old issues of *Pravda* that had
arrived the day before by a Soviet merchant ship.

The sound of footsteps in the hallway distracted her for a few seconds. She recognized Vidali's voice when he cursed because the lock was
stuck. The door opened, and the two looked at each other without saying
hello. Vidali threw a package on the table, some bread and some cans of
meat and sardines. He went over to her and put a bottle of wine in front
of her, waiting for a reaction, at least a vague smile of surprise. But she
just glanced at him, nodded, and went back to her reading.

He shrugged, muttered something, and took off his heavy leather
jacket, unfastened the cartridge belt, removed the two clips from the
belt, and laid them on the small table. Then he took out the large auto-

matic Astra and with a few quick movements disarmed it, removed the
bullet from the barrel, and began to dismantle and clean it. Looking inside the barrel against the light he said disinterestedly, "That fellow from
last night . . . Yes, the American photographer . . ."

He left the sentence dangling, concentrating on pouring a few drops
of oil on the small piece of cloth he had inserted in the opening. Without
raising her head, Modotti murmured, "Robert Capa?"

"Yes, him," Vidali responded, pushing the cloth in and out. "I saw
that he was very insistent. What was his problem?"

"If he has problems, I'm not interested," she answered. "He only
wanted to know why in the middle of this mess, I haven't picked up my
camera again."

Vidali let out a small sarcastic laugh and, in the meantime, removed
the bullets one after another, checking the spring of the clip with his
thumb.

"Of course—someone like him has found everything he was looking
for here. A good war with a pile of cadavers to immortalize. He will make
a nice pile of money, I imagine."

Modotti turned to look at him. She sighed and said, "You don't know
Robert Capa."

"That doesn't interest me either," Vidali retorted, standing up. He
went to look in a drawer, found a corkscrew, and uncorked the bottle of
red wine.

"They are all the same," he continued. "Boring bourgeois who find a
way to earn money at the expense of the people who die, and they come
all the way here to find a handful of cheap emotions! Hemingway—Dos
Passos—Malraux—for every massacre witnessed they will write a nice
little story that will sell a million copies."

He filled two glasses: He emptied his all at once and handed the other
one to her. He leaned over so that she would have to look directly at him.

"Of course. I forgot that you have always been so vulnerable to the
fascination of *culture*."

Modotti stared at him defiantly.

"Vittorio, how strange it is to hear you talk about the 'people who
die.'"

He tensed up and looked at her, waiting for her to continue. She picked up a newspaper on the table and showed him the front page. Vidali glanced at the headlines, then looked at her again, puzzled.

"All right, I'll read you the rest," she exclaimed. "The entire nation is fuming with indignation! And I, representative of the Department of the Public Prosecutor, join my indignant voice with the enraged voices of millions of men. I ask that those rabid dogs, those despicable pygmies and clowns, those dwarf dogs that trumpet like elephants, those unpleasant creatures, be executed at once!"

Vidali poured himself another glass of wine. He looked surprised and said, laughing, "Big, kind words indeed."

"They are Vyshinski's, the public prosecutor, and you know them better than I, since Vyshinski is one of the men that you most admire lately."

"No, I don't admire him. He does a job that I don't like. But right now we need men like him."

Modotti let out a bitter laugh and added, "At any rate, at one time you certainly admired those he is executing one after the other. Or have you forgotten?"

Vidali shrugged and sat back down on the bed. He carefully loaded the pistol again, ran the cartridge clip a few times, cursed the rust that had clogged the front sight, and muttered to himself, "Not even as an iron would I want it; the Nagant I had in Moscow was better. Three shots less, but certain."

"In the event that you need it urgently, use mine," Modotti said with a touch of irony in her voice, and she pointed to the other small table.

Vidali pretended not to hear her and, looking around him, said, "I have seen nasty hotels, but this one deserves special mention."

She closed the newspaper and put it back on top of the stack next to the table. Then she looked at him with a strange smile.

"And where would you like to mention it? In your memoirs?"

"Why not? I have a lot to tell, maybe too much, but it's still early. I still have many chapters to finish and just as many more to begin."

He got up, yawning, stretched, and stood looking out the window in front of him for a few seconds. His expression changed slowly, as if some thought made the forced happiness of a few seconds ago disappear.

"Tina—"

She quickly turned around, realizing from his tone that he was about to say something very serious.

"That sort of Mexican poet—Octavio Paz, that novice who goes around with his wife saying a lot of foolish things in public—"

"He is not a 'sort of' poet. He wrote *No Pasarán*, which is found in half the world," said Modotti dryly.

"Yes, what a pity that he is a bit confused about what is going on here."

"You wouldn't want to—"

"I don't want to do anything at all. It is you who should talk to him. Furthermore, since you met his wife in Mexico, it would be better to talk to her first. You should explain to her that the situation is much more complicated than they think, and that it would be advisable for them to stop associating with dangerous people."

A few days later Modotti met Elena Garro in the headquarters of Red Aid in Valencia. The wife of Octavio Paz seemed alarmed; she searched Modotti's face looking for an explanation, but she did not dare ask the reason for the ominous meeting. A man had approached Garro in a café, identifying himself as an agent of the intelligence service, and he had told her to accompany him to that office, where a *Mexican* friend wanted to talk to her.

Modotti greeted her politely and invited her to sit down. She asked if she remembered her; she spoke with some regret about Mexico and people they both knew; she tried hard to make the meeting seem like a simple chat between two women who hadn't seen each other in awhile. But Garro grew more and more restless. She had known Modotti only casually and they had never associated, making the familiarity she used with her now excessive. She seemed to take her time so as not to immediately confront the real reason for which she had ordered her there. During a moment of uncomfortable silence, Garro found the courage to ask her straight out: "Why did you send that policeman and not come to see me, if you knew very well where you could find Octavio and me?"

Modotti looked up and pursed her lips, looking for an answer. Then, letting out a long sigh, she said softly, "He wasn't a policeman. He was a comrade who works with me. And I didn't go to that location because the *problem* that I wanted to talk to you about has to do precisely with that."

Garro frowned, not believing what she had just heard.

"Yes, Elena, I am referring to the people who you see there, and who you probably regard as *compañeros* like the others. You and Octavio are associating with dubious characters, and without knowing it you relate details about our common struggle to individuals who have shown themselves to be traitors."

Garro turned pale. She moved her lips to reply, but in the end she only managed a smile, shaking her head and waving her hand as if dismissing an absurd idea.

"Traitors," she muttered. "Traitors like Andrés Nin, right?"

Modotti looked away, lit a cigarette and, just as she did so, remembered to offer one to Garro, who refused and added, "Where did Andrés Nin end up?"

Modotti made a slight grimace and murmured distractedly, "According to what they say, he was taken away by Nazi agents disguised as militiamen."

"Please don't repeat for me what the Party newspapers say. Not even you have the courage to say that Nin sold himself to the fascists."

"I don't know about that, Elena. And there are things that I don't want to know either. I decided to talk to you so that you and your husband don't end up embroiled in matters that you can't understand. Unfortunately a civil war produces wounds that are difficult to explain to someone who has never lived through certain realities."

Garro continued to look at her, and her earlier astonishment transformed into a deep sadness in her face.

"We cannot allow," Modotti went on, "the adventurous spirit of some people to compromise the course of the war. And what at other times would only be irresponsibility in this situation can represent real treason."

"Ana María would have committed treason too?" Garro asked in a suddenly harsh tone.

Modotti looked at her as if she were searching her memory for that name.

"Yes, Ana María Barón," the other woman continued. "A girl who was working as an interpreter. She was the one who accompanied the European delegates of the commission that investigated Nin's disappearance."

"I'm sorry. I've never heard of her."

"I hope not, because Ana María disappeared a few days ago, and she also used to go to the café that your *compañero* pulled me out of."

"I give you my word I don't know anything," Modotti said, wringing her hands nervously. "But don't take this as a warning. I am not threatening you, believe me. We suspect that those people are planning sabotage, and I wanted you and Octavio to know. That's all."

Garro suddenly stood up and mumbled, "All right, all right. Thank you for helping me understand many things."

Twenty-Three

The photographer and companion of Robert Capa, Gerda Taro, died at the front, crushed beneath the treads of a tank. David Seymour, another reporter who had tried in vain to convince Modotti to take up photography again, left Spain at the end of the war to later document new horrors and atrocities. He would die in 1956 during the Anglo-French invasion of the Suez Canal. Robert Capa would end his days in Vietnam in 1954, shooting his last photograph just before stepping on a land mine.

"I hate war," Modotti said one day, as she and Vidali looked at piles of debris that contained limbs of crushed human beings. "And nevertheless I would like to see another. I would like to see every country that has caused this and allowed it to happen to be reduced to this."

She rarely poured out her emotions about the war, and never in front of strangers. Only in one instance, during a lunch at the Soviet Embassy, did she express in public her resentment toward certain comrades who had always condemned her for her behavior. She did so taking her cue from comments that someone had made about Alexandra Kollontai,

whom Modotti had met in Mexico when she was ambassador of the Soviet Union:

> She is a formidable woman with a character and personality that I will
> never forget. She laughed when she spoke to me about some friends who
> had made her believe that I did not have a very good reputation in the
> capital—and not just for posing nude for Weston and Rivera. She also
> told me what they used to say about her when she was young, and
> proudly added that she had always done what she thought was right,
> without worrying about criticism. . . . Her private life was her business.
> Just like mine is my business.

Vidali was surprised by the vehement reaction from Modotti, who
usually remained silent, especially in situations like that, with high officials of the Comintern and diplomats seated at the same table. Also present was General Berzin, known as Grisha in Spain, the one who in 1932
had proposed that Modotti enter the secret service.

After the bloody Battle of Jarama, Modotti was sent to Málaga, where the
Francoist advance necessitated the city's evacuation. She arrived in
Almería with Dr. Norman Bethune and found the city in total chaos: Aerial bombings came in waves every half hour; the streets were full of
refugees; ships shelled the port from the sea, and on land Italian tanks
encircled the meager defenses and machine-gunned civilians who fled.

When she returned to Valencia, Modotti found a climate of open hos-
tility: The people accused the government and the General Staff of having abandoned Málaga to its fate, of having neglected that sector of the
front despite having known about the Francoist offensive well in advance. The massive movement of Italian troops could not go unnoticed,
and the people wanted to know why the Republican army had not attempted any defense.

In Guadalajara, on the other hand, the fascists were crushingly defeated in a confrontation that saw hand-to-hand battles between Italians
from the two opposing armies. After days and nights of tending to the
wounded who arrived from the front, Doctor Bethune was persuaded to
leave Spain. Whoever took the final outcome for granted preferred that

Bethune's international reputation be used to support new causes. The Canadian physician would die in China, where he had been transferred in order to organize a field hospital following the Maoist troops.

In September 1937 Vidali was sent on a mission to Paris, where he managed to elude the Deuxième Bureau. When he returned to Spain, he saw Modotti again in Barcelona, where there was a climate of expectation of an imminent defeat. The isolated victory in Teruel did not raise hopes. Asturias was doomed, and the imminent offensive would take the Francoists from Caspe to the sea, dividing the Republican territory in half. Valencia and Barcelona were subjected to incessant bombings; the mass exodus had begun.

Modotti traveled to Valencia in a small boat across a strip of sea patrolled by Falangist coast guard vessels. Despite her fatigue and sense of hopelessness, she insisted on embarking against the wishes of Vidali, who tried in vain to convince her not to. Miraculously, she arrived at her destination: the motor had been damaged and she had barely avoided landing in enemy territory.

Until the summer of 1938, Modotti had worked as an editor of the newspaper *Ayuda*, the organ of Spanish Red Aid. In November, after a rough trip, she arrived in Madrid to take part in the National Solidarity Congress: a name that sounded tragically paradoxical considering that two months before, Juan López Negrín's government had accepted the dissolution of the International Brigades during the meeting of the League of Nations, convened in Geneva on September 23. The withdrawal of the foreign volunteers would be ratified later by the Munich Pact among Hitler, Mussolini, Chamberlain, and Daladier, which would help transform part of Czechoslovakia into a German "protectorate."

The Republican counteroffensive on the Ebro River provided a brief respite for the besieged Spanish capital. The departure of the International Brigades thus became the symbol of capitulation to the will of the new European order, but authorities organized a sad parade of volunteers, who marched before the ministers and generals receiving a kind of official appreciation for their work. Modotti was also in that reviewing box, next to the political commissioner "Carlos Contreras."

"It's not fair for it to end like this," she said to him when they returned to the hotel. "We have struggled for almost three years. I have seen fighters from every battle, maimed and wounded, march with bundles of flowers and the flag. They had tears in their eyes and great sadness on their faces. My heart sank with the thought that this was really the end."

The afternoon of the final day of the congress, Madrid was attacked by a savage aerial and artillery bombardment. Vidali was among the wounded. Modotti spent the night going from one hospital to another, identifying bodies of unknown people and expecting each time to find herself before the body of "Carlos." Instead she would see him again on a stretcher, dazed and battered, but not unable to curse his bad luck: A wall had collapsed on him just as he was taking cover.

With his head bandaged and one arm in a sling, Vidali showed up to report to Togliatti. When Togliatti saw the condition he was in, he burst out laughing, causing Dolores Ibarruri, *La Pasionaria*, and General Lister also to start laughing. This time the cynicism of "Comrade Ercoli" was not shared by Vidali, who became very angry. Many years later he would recall the episode with these words: "When I was injured, many others had lost their lives. As for me, I was bothered by their laughter, and even offended."

After a three-week recovery period, he went to Albacete with Modotti, and then they flew by plane to Barcelona. Half an hour after taking off, they had to turn around because of radio trouble. But no sooner had they begun the trip again when they were intercepted by Francoists in Fiats who forced them to land in a field near the city. During the machine-gunning phase, Modotti had remained impassive to such an extent that the crew members praised her, amazed by her coolness.

On December 31 the final offensive targeted Barcelona, which would fall on January 25. "María" was ordered to make frequent trips to France to accompany wounded Party militants or important people who needed to reach safety on the other side of the border. Transferred to Figueras, she was miraculously unharmed when Red Aid headquarters was the target of a bomb.

The Mexican intellectual Fernando Gamboa was one of the last to leave Spain. After their previous encounter at the congress in Valencia, he again saw Modotti casually.

I was told that an important collection of films and records had been abandoned in the castle in Figueras. The Mexican Embassy had allowed us to use an official car, and my wife and I left immediately. There had been a massive bombardment the previous day, because the latest Courts of the Second Spanish Republic were assembling precisely in Figueras; and so the people fleeing Barcelona had found themselves underneath the bombs in their desperate attempt to reach France. When we arrived at the castle, an enormous Gothic building, we discovered that the material was not what we were looking for: There were stacks of films, but all were new. It was a small storage facility and not the archives that I had imagined. I then headed for the town, which was twenty minutes away by car, but found nothing as it was almost completely abandoned. As I crossed through the deserted town center, I saw a woman sitting at the table of an outdoor café, alone and motionless. It was Tina Modotti. When she recognized me she smiled. I asked her what she was doing in that absurd place which was on the verge of becoming a ghost town. "I'm waiting," she responded. Then we hugged, and she explained to me that the retreating army would pass through there and, therefore, so would Vidali. I tried to make her understand that she was taking a big risk waiting for the remainder of an army that was falling back under Francoist attacks; I proposed to take her in half an hour to Agullana in our car bearing diplomatic flags, and finally I attempted to joke with her saying, "We aren't in Mexico, and you can't enlist as a soldier's aide." But she was not convinced.

We left her at the small table around six in the afternoon, in the cold February sun that illuminated the lines of peasants who were fleeing through the mountains, and she, all alone, with that penetrating look of hers and that pensive expression. . . . The image of an exhausted woman, who was carrying inside the anguish of the defeated, closed up in her melancholy solitude.

Half a million refugees left Catalonia under an icy rain that had begun to fall without interruption during the final days of the retreat; they fled, pursued by bombardments that offered no respite, without provisions and facing a future without hope. The only ones who defended the civilians who escaped were the few international volunteers who had refused to obey the dissolution order, and the Catalonian anarchists who for many years would continue their guerrilla warfare from the Pyrenees.

Modotti said good-bye to Matilde Landa, her closest friend in those tragic months. Landa had decided to stay. She wanted to fight with the resistance on the last front, that of the center-south. She would be captured by the Francoists in the fall of Madrid and sentenced to death. Her sentence was commuted to life imprisonment thanks to the intervention of many notable foreign figures, and she would endure six months of torture in the underground chambers of the police. A few years later she "fell" out of a window at the prison in Majorca. Her husband, Paco Ganivet, after having obtained permission to return from exile, would take his own life in Madrid, throwing himself out of a fifth-story window.

Modotti resigned herself to following the long line of ragged men and women, heads down, who dropped their weapons and submitted to the checkpoints of the not-so-kind guards on the French border. She had no problems: She had a fake passport with a visa from the Consulate of France in the name of Carmen Ruiz Sánchez; she had already crossed the border several times with it in the previous months.

Part Five

A KIND OF

HOMECOMING

Twenty-Four

The French Communists' reception of the Spanish refugees was no warmer than the government's. They were veterans of a war that everyone wanted to forget and, what is more, they created huge problems for the already unstable balance of a country that had just lived through the disastrous experience of Léon Blum's Popular Front. Modotti felt obligated to confront this reality, inconceivable for her, of the troubled and disdainful reaction of some militants to the requests of the exiles. From Perpignan she went to the Casa del Pueblo, where she had a run-in with a guard whose attitude was anything but friendly. Vidali's angry reaction to her treatment sparked off an incident that would end up in the secretariat of the French Communist Party. They left there very late in the evening, running the risk of encountering the police, who were looking for the defeated close to the border, and they sought refuge in the Spanish consulate. Seeing that it was already full of people, they decided to go to a hotel where other friends of theirs were staying.

Dawn came amid interminable discussions and resentments fed by the doubts about the role that Moscow had really played in Spain, overcome by the bitter awareness of belonging to a chapter in history that was already closed. Only Vidali continued to show a trace of optimism that went beyond the situation of the moment, certain as he was of having carried out his mission and of still having many more cards to play in the future. Modotti listened in silence, absorbed in her mute resignation.

On the train to Paris, Modotti and Vidali reviewed the instructions on the work that awaited them at the French branch of Red Aid. They had received the order not to return to Spain for any reason, but they also were given the mission of coordinating the control of the refugees who were coming to the organization by the thousands. They stayed at the home of the lawyer Marcel Williard, and they got to work without losing a single day. In their first meeting, Tina was struck by the outburst of a Parisian delegate, who did not beat around the bush, stating, "The Spanish refugees have lost their war, and now they can't expect much from us." Overcome by his rage, he shouted, "And you have lost the war against Nazism! Get it into your heads that the defeat of Spain is the beginning of the end of antifascism in all of Europe!" Vidali did not interrupt, and the French Communist put an end to the matter with a shrug of his shoulders.

Another tough blow for Modotti was the death of poet Antonio Machado. Gravely ill, he had crossed the border on foot in heavy rain. Pneumonia would end his life soon after. Modotti went to Colliure and found him already at the point of death. After his death, she sank into a deep depression that would begin to lift only after she made a drastic decision: She wanted to return to Italy to fight secretly against the regime. More than a political choice, hers was a desperate search for a dramatic epilogue.

Like all Italians who had lived in the Soviet Union, Modotti, too, was prohibited from returning, under any circumstances, to Italy. Guiseppe di Vittorio spent his days talking with her about this, trying to make her see all the negative aspects of her decision, and to understand how isolated she could feel once she broke ties with the Comintern. Modotti finally gave up her adventurous attitude and decided to remain in France, where at that time there was plenty of work to be done. But a few days later, English Communist representative Tom Bell arrived in Paris with an assignment for Vidali and Tina from Elena Stasova: They were to go to the United States, officially to "coordinate the arrival of other Spanish refugees." But first they could return to Moscow if they chose, to enjoy a "deserved rest period."

Entering the United States illegally and with fake visas involved the risk of being identified and detained. But Modotti did not hesitate; she considered the Soviet Union to be an even greater danger, as she recalled the climate of suspicion that had surrounded her during the last few months she had lived there. At any rate, to continue to declare herself a Communist was more important to her than fear of the paranoid delirium that had been unleashed in Moscow.

Vidali arrived in New York on March 23, 1939. Having decided to travel separately, Modotti embarked on the *Queen Mary* three weeks later, carrying her passport in the name of Carmen Ruiz Sánchez, which contained a visa valid for only three months. When she presented it to Immigration and Naturalization authorities, she had the bitter surprise of discovering that they had already been informed of her arrival. But this time they chose not to call attention to the matter. There were no press or photographers, nor was she detained: They invited her to leave immediately for Veracruz.

After nine years of illusions and disillusions that had finally run dry, Modotti returned to Mexico. Vidali stayed in the United States for a while, but he would soon join her. In fact, his new mission consisted of verifying certain contacts in Mexico City, where the delicate job of weaving the invisible spiderweb around the objective had already begun. Surrounded by the utmost secrecy, the mission came directly from Stalin, who had asked that only the most loyal agents be chosen.

One year later Leon Trotsky was granted political asylum by the president of the Mexican republic, Lázaro Cárdenas, and he moved definitively to the capital with his wife and a few loyal supporters who also served as his bodyguards.

On April 19, 1939, Tina saw pass before her eyes the majestic fortress of San Juan de Ulúa, the swarm of colors on the wharf, the interminable line of boats in the bay . . . and the heavy air, thick with humidity, the blinding sun that made the hunched backs at the stern of the boats glisten with sweat, the absurdly blue sky, an intense cobalt . . . and the sounds, the voices, the strong aromas of Veracruz.

Confused, she walked, in the middle of the noisy crowd, all around the wharf with uncertain, tremulous steps after her long journey. She smiled faintly, absently, at the little children who hurried to pick up the little luggage she had.

The plaza was enclosed by arcades, with tables and chairs stacked up, waiting for yet another sleepless night to fall, amid cases of beer and omnipresent marimbas. With her eyes of a century ago she again saw the anxious face of Edward, fascinated and lost, impatient because of the heat, and overcome by a contagious frenzy. His panting, because of the weight of the heavy Graflex and tripod he carried on his back, the indecision before so many stimuli. Burning eyes, filled with an irrepressible energy. Their young eyes reflected in the water of the fountain in the middle of the plaza.

She sat on the stone curb, looking at the white walls, wondering if she had ever really lived all this, if those faraway days filled with dreams had belonged to her. She stuck her hand in the tepid water, turned around and noticed her aged face, her sunken and dead eyes, her lips puckered with sadness. The *past* did not exist, she thought. It didn't exist because it had passed. And now the future didn't exist either. She was left with only the impalpable present, fragile, with the same consistency as her image reflected in the trembling water of the fountain.

She passed her wet hand across her face. Her eyes met those of the children who were waiting patiently, the suitcases balanced on their heads, not asking her anything. Maybe they were thinking that the foreigner was very tired after a long journey.

In Mexico City, Modotti stayed in the San Angel area at a house that belonged to friends of Vidali, who would join her a few days later. He was still using the alias Carlos Contreras, a history professor born in La Coruña, Spain. Red Aid saw to it that Modotti received a small stipend with which she could support herself for at least the first few months. The Mexican ambassador in Madrid, Adalberto Tejeda, interceded so that the government would revoke Modotti's deportation order, and Carmen Ruiz Sánchez became, once again, Assunta Modotti, although in her reduced circle of friends she was still called María. She rented a tiny apartment in a modest neighborhood at 137 Doctor Balmis Street, a few minutes from the historic center. It was actually an *azotea*, practically an attic converted into a living space, at the top of a three-story house. From the terrace the volcanoes and the bell tower of the cathedral were visible, but the two narrow rooms, filled with humidity from the rain coming in through cracks, had very little in common with the houses in which she had lived previously.

Modotti immediately looked for work as a translator, and Vidali obtained an excellent assignment as a journalist for *El Popular*, a newspaper with ties to the Mexican Communist community. But the political "rest period" was not destined to last long. Modotti had to return to New York to evaluate the possibility of a new and longer stay for Vidali in the United States, where they had instructed him to work closely with the leader of the Communist Party, Earl Browder. This time she would manage to pass unnoticed, emphasizing her humble appearance as a woman older than she really was: from the photos on her identification card, nobody would recognize the "beautiful Italian revolutionary" the American newspapers had talked about years before. But nevertheless, the FBI would soon open a file on her based on a "confidential report" sent by the Consulate General of the United States in Mexico City, in which she was described as an "agent of the Soviet secret service."

She stayed in New York for approximately two months and, when she returned, she told Vidali that they considered his immediate transfer to be "too dangerous." The order from Earl Browder was for him not to move from Mexico, at least for the time being, and to proceed with the work already begun.

Twenty-Five

D iego Rivera and Frida Kahlo were at the port in Tampico on January 9, 1937, to welcome Trotsky. Thanks to Rivera's intervention, President Cárdenas had granted him political asylum. In constant fear of an attack by Stalinist agents, Trotsky's group traveled surrounded by an entourage of armed men and by a cordon of policemen.

The first residence of the exiled "prophet" was the *casa azul* of Frida Kahlo, and a rumor immediately began to circulate about a presumed relationship between them. It was true that Kahlo was attracted to Trotsky's unsuspected sensibility, and she spent hours and hours on the patio talking to the living legend, whom she, with simple innocence, called "El Viejo." They would also exchange affectionate letters filled with mutual admiration that Kahlo later gave back to him when the somewhat surprised, somewhat amused gossip of friends threatened to reach the ears of the extremely jealous Rivera. As for Trotsky's companion, Natalia Sedova, she too noticed Trotsky's interest in the young painter. But that childish attraction was not enough to ruin the relationship of a lifetime. Obviously Kahlo was not well liked by Sedova, especially after the latter read the dedication that Kahlo had written to him on the back of the self-portrait she had given him: "To Leon Trotsky with all my love, November 7, 1937."

Apart from this, Kahlo and Rivera's house did not provide all the security requirements that the situation demanded. In January 1938, three years after the disappearance of his son, Sergei, Trotsky received the tragic news of the death of his other son, Liova. The GPU was eliminating the people he most loved one after another; unable to create a political void around Trotsky, Stalin tried to conquer his stubborn resistance by killing his children. His tight circle of collaborators and security guards persuaded him to choose a residence that was easier to defend against possible direct attacks. In the same suburb of Coyoacán, there was a huge house with a very tall wall at 45 Viena Street: two adjoining single-story buildings and a large front entrance that cars could enter made it possible to come and go without getting out of the car. After a few months of work, it was transformed into a small fortress. There were parapets, turrets, peepholes, bars on the windows, and small, armored, missileproof doors in order to hinder an assault. Shifts at the "bastions" were organized among the trusted guardians, men who had come from Europe and the United States to join him and defend him at any cost. They were Otto Schüssler, Walter Kerley, Charles Cornell, Jake Cooper, and Harold Robbins, who acted as "coordinator." Also among these men was Robert Sheldon Harte, whose role as either unknowing victim or probable traitor would remain unclear.

The beautiful garden, full of flowers and cacti, would become the only place where Trotsky could safely spend time outdoors, talking with visitors who were carefully screened by his men, or tirelessly reading publications and reports from all corners of the world. He spent the rest of the day in his study, using his Dictaphone to record his endless memories and analyses of the present and the future.

But the meticulous precautions and constant surveillance did not prevent twenty assailants from entering the garden through the garage door on the night of May 23, 1940. Brief but intense shooting erupted before the defenders, whose reaction was quick and decisive, were able to drive back the intruders in just a few minutes. Leading the attackers was Siqueiros, who managed to introduce the barrel of his Thompson machine gun into the window of the room where Trotsky and his wife were sleeping. But the windowsill was too high, and Siqueiros had to shoot without aiming. The burst of fire destroyed the walls, grazing the bed, behind which the elderly couple had thrown themselves when they heard the first shots. The assailants withdrew with no losses and certain that they had achieved their goal, giving up their fight against the men who responded to the firing from every door and window. In the end only little Vsevolod Volkow, Trotsky's grandson, the son of his oldest daughter, Zina, was injured; a ricocheting bullet had grazed his foot. The bombs, scattered throughout the garden and in front of the door, were deactivated before they exploded.

In the following days the theory would take shape that there must have been an accomplice inside the house who had allowed the assailants to enter the garden. Sheldon's disappearance lent more credence to the theory that there could have been a traitor who had left the front door open or even led the commandos to Trotsky's room. Investigations led to the arrest of some members of the group, who during the interrogations eventually revealed Siqueiros's name. The other man responsible for the attack was a stranger with a foreign accent who seemed to have played the role of facilitator, maintaining contact with whoever was providing the information and giving orders from time to time.

During the search for evidence at a house Siqueiros had bought in Desierto de los Leones, a hilly area located a few kilometers from the capital, Sheldon's body was found in the kitchen, buried hastily under the beaten-soil floor. Trotsky could not hold back his tears before the body of the young man. It may have been the only time the old commander of the Red Army was seen crying in public. He was indignant at the suggestion that Sheldon could have betrayed him. Moreover, he immediately ordered a marble tablet to be engraved in memory of his sacrifice and placed on the wall at the entrance to the garden.

Siqueiros was accused of having shot him twice in the back of the neck. It was not known if Sheldon was an accomplice or the victim of an abduction, but what was clear was that he had had to be silenced in order to eliminate a dangerous witness. In this way no one would be able to reveal the identity of the mysterious "messenger" with the foreign accent. Siqueiros's arrest would not help to clarify things: He was so well regarded and respected that the government provided him with a residence where anyone could visit him and from which he never stopped sending "advice" and recommendations to ministers and generals, frequent visitors to that unique "prison."

"Can you at least tell me where you're going?" Vidali asked nervously. Leaning against the doorjamb, he watched her, incredulous, as she quickly packed the little clothing she had in a torn leather suitcase. After a great effort to close and lock it, Modotti looked him up and down, as if she were upset.

"What have you come here for?"

Vidali shrugged. "I came to see how you were, and I find you with your suitcase ready to leave without even letting me know."

"Don't worry," she said with a mocking smile, "I have no intention of 'disappearing.'"

Vidali went over to her and gently took her by the arms. Modotti broke free with a jerk.

"Maybe something has happened that—"

"No, please!" she exclaimed, almost shouting. "Nothing at all has happened. Everything is under control, right?"

Vidali looked impatient.

"Come on. You aren't going to believe the despicable things that they have been saying—"

"I don't believe anything anymore. It's been a long time since I have believed in something or someone. But you can't pretend that you don't see or feel."

"Listen, Tina, David has organized all this without relying on anyone, I couldn't imagine that—"

"You couldn't imagine? But you have been paving the way for months! Your pseudonyms don't work with me: You have led the campaign against that poor old man, you have written dozens and dozens of articles in order to portray him as the worst surviving enemy. And now that a group of scoundrels has carried out the heroic act that we were all waiting for, you come to me to say that you couldn't have imagined it!"

"There is a huge difference between writing for a newspaper and shooting at him."

"Save it. I know you well enough to know that he wasn't able to organize everything alone. He is fanatical enough to do it, but not intelligent enough to lead it."

Vidali folded his arms and looked at her provocatively.

"In that case, it wouldn't have ended the way it did, right?"

"Yes," Modotti replied angrily, "I know that they regard you as a
guarantee. In addition to the propaganda, they should have made you
lead the operation. You have never fallen short of any objective, right?
Nice work—an injured little boy and a poor fellow with two bullets in the
back of his neck. Now you can also write an article on the bravery of
your butchers."

"Be careful with your emotions. I hope you aren't so imprudent as to
go around saying such nonsense."

She stopped. She dropped her suitcase on the floor and stared at Vidali, who was lighting a cigarette without taking his eyes off her.

"I don't want to have anything to do with you or with those like you,"
she said, trembling. "But what I think and feel I keep to myself. As I have
always done."

Vidali nodded and gestured with his hand as if to say that he didn't
doubt it. She went back to looking for something in the closet, cursing
under her breath.

"Then it's final," he said after a while, changing his tone, "the decision not to renew your membership card."

"If you need an excuse for your *compañeros*, you can also say that the
residency permit prevents me from carrying out political activities. Remind them of the Mexican law concerning it, and do it in such a way so
that they forget I exist."

She went to the kitchen and rummaged around in the cabinet, knocking over a few glasses, while Vidali watched her, worried.

"There is something else you can do: Forget about me once and for
all, and marry Isabel. I know that she expects nothing less. She worships
you like a god, and she will be happy to give you that child that you want
so much."

She threw her head back, letting out a burst of icy laughter.

"The heir of Comandante Carlos! He could only be a hero—"

"Isabel is just a good friend," Vidali interrupted her, stopping at the door and preventing her from returning to the room. "As you too were at one time."

She looked at him with disdain and replied, "At one time I was blind and deaf. Today, at most, I can remain silent."

She pushed him aside and went to a corner of the room where there was an old mimeograph machine. She picked up a bundle of papers and handed them to Vidali.

"You take them to headquarters. And if you want to print more, take this machine and have someone else do it. The neighbors can't take the squeaking, day and night, any longer."

"Are you saying that you won't even be seen at the Party?"

She sat down on the bed with a sigh of fatigue.

"With what I had to swallow the other day," she muttered, shaking her head, "any effort is futile. And if you want me to be any clearer, you have all tired me out."

"That's enough, Tina. You're only looking for excuses!" Vidali exclaimed, banging the wall.

"*Excuses?!*" she shouted. "To become an ally of Nazi Germany is to spit on the dead, on the sacrifices of an entire generation. For you, all this is just a diplomatic problem, isn't that right?"

"You stop at appearances and you aren't able to see things as a whole. That has always been your problem."

Modotti got up, took a few slow steps toward him, stopped a few centimeters from his face, and whispered, "As you see the whole, is there also room for those two or three hundred German Communists whom Stalin returned to Hitler as a sign of friendship?"

Vidali moved away, turning his back to her, and went out to the terrace. But she followed him and continued, "Hundreds of men and women who have ended up with ropes around their necks, their lives used as gifts, as goods to be traded between murderers of the same race."

"What the devil do you know?!" Vidali shouted, turning around abruptly. He pushed her inside and closed the door. "It's all propaganda, rumors that those like you have spread. Were you there, perchance? Did you see that they were handed over to the Nazis? Do you have proof of what you are saying?"

"Proof . . . ," she said with a bitter smile before freeing herself.

She picked up her jacket off the bed and folded it over her arm. She picked up her suitcase and went to open the door. Vidali fell back, putting his back against the door, blocking her way.

"Are you coming back?" he asked.

"Yes, of course. Where do you want me to go?"

"When?"

She rubbed her forehead and brushed some hair out of her face.

"I don't know . . . in two or three months, I think."

"And if I should need to talk to you, where can I find you?"

She sighed and looked at him, resigned.

"I have been offered a good job: to illustrate a book with my photographs. It is by Constancia de la Mora; you know her too. She has gathered material on the people of Oaxaca, and she wants to go back there with me to take the photos. We will be traveling constantly—and, anyway, I don't know why you would need to talk to me."

Vidali stepped aside and let her leave. Modotti crossed the terrace and, when she reached the front door, turned and said, "You can sleep peacefully, Vittorio. With the few friends I still have left, I only talk about photographs—and about other foolishness that of course has nothing to do with you. But don't count on me for help anymore. For *anything*."

Twenty-Six

"'F ate' has granted me a respite. It will be short-lived," Leon Trotsky wrote on May 24, 1940. And only three months later, on August 20, Ramón Mercader del Río killed him, shattering his skull with a pickax.

Preparations for the attack were so complex that only after many years of investigation would it be possible to reconstruct the plot. Even the real name of the assassin would not be discovered until several months after his capture. The plan was devised in New York, where the thread that held together the tangle of relationships and complicities began to unravel. The Communist leader Earl Browder entrusted Jack Stachel, GPU agent, to put Mercader in touch with someone who could introduce him into the select circle of people who visited Trotsky. The first link in the chain was journalist Ruby Weil, who was trusted among Trotskyites but who actually worked for a Comintern official. Through her, Mercader met Silvia Agelov, the sister of one of Trotsky's secretaries. That meeting took place in Paris, where the hired assassin had the use of an apartment rented by Siqueiros in the summer of 1938. At that time a banal "incident" threatened to force them to change the plan. Octavio

Paz, who had just returned from Spain, ran into Siqueiros by chance while walking down the street in the French capital. Siqueiros was so ill at ease that it aroused the suspicions of Paz, who could not understand his uneasiness when he asked him why he had left Lister's division. Siqueiros knew the Mexican poet's feelings with respect to Stalinism and feared that the next day, mission accomplished, he would figure out the real reason for Siqueiros's presence in Paris. There was no doubt that his temperament was well suited to the duties of a troop officer or to leading a commando squad of assailants, but he was not cold-blooded enough to control any unexpected situation. Seeing Paz's surprised smile, he jabbered some broken sentences, trying to find some credible excuse. Finally he said that he was just passing through France and was headed to Italy to carry out a mission related to the war in Spain. He even went as far as to ask Paz to accompany him to the Gare de Lyon, hoping that this would dispel any doubts. Then he got on the first train headed for Turin by way of Switzerland.

Siqueiros thought that his performance had been convincing enough not to compromise the success of the operation. Nevertheless Paz had the impression that Siqueiros had made up the trip to Italy as he went along in order to hide the real reason for his "passing through" Paris, and that he would get off that train at the first stop. Despite his fears, however, this would not lead him to denounce Siqueiros.

Silvia Agelov was in the French capital to attend a congress in which Trotsky himself was taking part, and on that occasion she met the Rosemers, long-time friends of Trotsky and frequent visitors to the house in Coyoacán. Agelov was a militant Labor Party member, and she had already been in Mexico in 1937, visiting her sister.

Ramón Mercader was an attractive, educated man who dressed stylishly and behaved with great discretion. His objective was to establish a relationship with Silvia, but he did not want to act hastily and risk someone becoming suspicious of him. On the contrary, he did everything he could to make their meetings appear casual; later he would let her be the one to contact him. The two saw each other again in the United States and then in Mexico. His cover as a businessman working in the importexport business justified his constant trips. He went by the name Frank Jackson, according to his falsified passport, which had previously belonged to the Canadian Communist Tony Babich, killed on the Madrid front.

Silvia Agelov fell in love with "Frank." They saw each other more and more frequently, and he invited her to accompany him on some "business" trips, perfectly designed so as to avoid any suspicions regarding his activities. She was now a common sight in the house-fortress on Viena Street, and Mercader limited his actions to accompanying her and waiting for her to come outside, with the goal of becoming a familiar figure to the guards stationed at the wall. As the months went by, the guards began to greet him in a friendly manner and kid around with him, but Mercader did nothing to force the situation. One day they invited Silvia on an excursion to a neighboring town located on the waters of Lake Xochimilco, and her boyfriend "Frank Jackson" was readily accepted into the group. From that point on there was no reason to make him wait in the street. When he went to pick Silvia up, they opened the small side door with the armored grating and let him into the garden. If he wanted, he could have gone into the house, but he avoided appearing pushy or curious. He walked around the garden filled with cacti and flowers without ever asking questions or showing any interest in the life of the inhabitants of the house or of their friends. He did not have to wait long to be invited for lunch or to have his first conversation with Trotsky, which was superficial and vague. In fact, during the excursion to Xochimilco, Mercader said only hello to him, and then got in a boat alone with Silvia.

But in the meantime Silvia's sister, who had returned for a while from New York, wrote Trotsky a letter warning him that the Stalinist agents Helman and Stachel would be arriving in the Mexican capital; a sign that was part of the habitual vigilance that the Trotskyites exercised over the movement of potential hired assassins.

After two years of working patiently, Mercader had achieved the proposed goal. To Trotsky he declared that he was apolitical, but he knew how to show a certain fascination for his ideas at the same time that he displayed an attitude of carefree mediocrity. He did not risk appearing false by showing the admiration everyone probably expected him to; on the contrary, he provoked Trotsky by defending the merits of capitalism using the simple interests of a businessman without being disagreeable.

His ignorance seemed sincere, and he was humble enough to recognize his own limits each time the inaccuracy of certain assertions came to his attention. He was a perfect nobody, and therefore he could be attracted by ideals that he did not understand. And when months later he showed a vague passion for writing and journalism, Trotsky spontaneously offered to correct some "fragments."

This would be the excuse that would allow him to enter the house-fortress alone, lock himself in the study with Trotsky, get him to focus his attention on reading a long article, and then move behind him and strike him silently with the pickax. He carried a .45 automatic in his pocket to use just in case.

But the plan to murder him without making the slightest noise and to leave the house calmly immediately afterward was hindered by the unexpected reaction of the victim: With his skull pierced and blood obscuring his vision, Trotsky threw himself on Mercader and bit down hard on the hand that had struck him. The armed secretaries came and immobilized Mercader, who was terrified before Trotsky's apparent invulnerability: The old Bolshevik soldier was now standing, pressing a handkerchief to the deep wound to try to stop the hemorrhaging and, helped by his wife, remained calm so that he could recount how everything had happened and advise Charles Cornell in English not to kill "Jackson": "We must make him talk; it's important to find out who he really is." Then he calmed Natalia Sedova, telling her that he felt better. But, returning to English so that she would not understand, he murmured to Cornell, "I'm sorry, it's really the end. This time they have done it to us."

When they transferred him to the hospital, he was still conscious. He died the next day, trying in vain to communicate something rendered indistinguishable by progressive paralysis.

While Modotti was detained on the *Queen Mary* and forced to continue on to Veracruz, Vidali remained in New York for a few days in order to meet with Browder and Stachel. Stachel traveled to Mexico City when preparations for the attack were already in the final phase. In mid-1939, Modotti returned to New York on Vidali's instructions, probably without knowing the real reason.

Carlos Contreras was entrusted, most importantly, with the press campaign against Trotsky and even went so far as to organize demonstrations outside the house in Coyoacán. Trotsky's assassination had to be carried out only after hatred and contempt for him had been roused in the political environment of the Mexican Communist Party, so local public opinion would consider it as the logical epilogue to that uproar. In the meantime, Vidali saw Siqueiros regularly, and Siqueiros protected his activity by taking advantage of those he knew inside the government; the two took part in the same cell meetings and in "business" dinners at the painter's house.

Modotti, on the other hand, moved away from militancy after her last mission in New York, and when they offered to renew her Party membership card, she declined, saying that she preferred not to defy the tacit agreement that had been reached with the Mexican authorities, which obligated political refugees not to interfere in the country's internal affairs. For her, 137 Doctor Balmis Street became a solitary refuge, her first real house after so many years of wandering in pursuit of an already defeated ideal. In what Vidali called "the hovel in the sky," with water leaking through the dilapidated roof in the rainy season and the sun that immediately turned it incandescently hot, she spent her days reading on the terrace in the shade of a trellis of climbing carnations with a cat and a little dog as her only company. Little by little she left political activity behind and dedicated herself to the solitary work of translating books so that she could earn a living. Her commitment was now limited to typing articles for the bulletin of the Garibaldi Antifascist Association. This was also a way of preserving a fragile relationship with Italy, for which she felt an increasingly painful nostalgia. She wrote, corrected proofs, and mimeographed, in a routine that wore her down day after day. She saw none of the people whom she had met in 1929, as she avoided any contact with those circles. One morning, as she was going into a post office in the city center, she exchanged looks with a man she recognized at once: It was Bruno Traven who, puzzled, searched his own memory for that face. She had changed a lot, but after hesitating a few seconds, Traven smiled openly and went to hug her. Modotti drew back, motioning with her hand as if to say that she couldn't talk and that she would call him later. Used to the rules of a semiunderground life, Traven stood still and pretended to address someone who was passing by. He would not see her again, much less get a phone call.

Why did she not even want to greet him? Did she do it just to avoid reliving memories that would now be painful for her, so she could escape regret for an era so far from the tragedies she had later lived through? Or perhaps it was her orders to keep quiet, obligating her not to renew any contact that could endanger matters, that forced her, against her will, to be a passive accomplice.

The few friends who went to visit her every now and then at the *azotea* amid the rooftops saw her age quickly. Although she retained the sweetness in her face and the depth of her look, the austere severity that her eyes at one time knew how to express had given way decisively to a desperate sadness. The mysterious charm, praised by all those who had known her ten years earlier, was replaced by the resigned expression in the last photos of her. Furthermore, economic difficulties forced her to suppress her passion for photography, which had never completely left her. Only in one case did she seem to recover the determination she once had, leaving her isolation to dedicate herself to the only activity that could give her the strength to break with the recent past: She moved for three months to the state of Oaxaca with the Spanish writer Constancia de la Mora. She lived several weeks in the remotest communities of the Sierra Madre, taking numerous photos of Indian women and their crafts, which reflected a very old sun-worshipping culture. But the book would never be completed because of Mora's death in a plane crash, and the photos were lost.

Twenty-Seven

In the early stages of the investigation, "Jackson" stated that his real name was Jacques Mornard, and that he was a Canadian citizen. Then he was Belgian and, finally, Soviet. Only when it was discovered that his mother, Caridad Mercader del Río, was Spanish would the origins of the Stalinist-hired assassin be clarified once and for all.

Caridad Mercader had first moved to Belgium and then to France, where her five children were raised. This explained Ramón Mercader's perfect French. Entering the ranks of the GPU through a "special cell" that operated in Paris in 1928 and that answered directly to the Soviet Embassy, she returned to Spain during the civil war, proving her blind fanaticism in various ways. Ramón then enlisted in the Communist militias in Catalonia, in which one of his brothers would die in combat. In 1940 his mother was transferred to Moscow and went to work in the office of Beria with the express order never to talk about her son Ramón: She had to lose track of him completely so that she could reinforce her new identity and erase entirely her previous life.

But Ramón Mercader's personality would not fulfill the expectations of those who believed him to be a cold and determined executor of orders. The closer he came to the goal of the operation, the more uncertainty and fear he showed. Witnesses spoke of some "distinguished gentlemen with foreign accents" who used to pick him up at his home in the Mexican capital and whose behavior toward him gave the impression that they wanted to support and encourage him, as if he had to carry out something he was trying to avoid. One of these encounters took a turn in which Mercader was overcome by rage and his "friends," alternating threats with promises and good manners, tried to get him to listen to "reason."

When Mercader could no longer maintain the appearance of the sympathizing Communist horrified by Trotsky's "anti-Soviet betrayal," he would admit having acted on behalf of the GPU—blackmailed in order to save the life of his mother, who was being held hostage in Moscow.

What relationship could there have been between the two attacks?

On the surface it seemed absurd that Siqueiros would attack the house in Coyoacán when a complicated plan prepared during two years of extremely delicate work was already under way. One explanation could have come from Mercader's rage: He was proving to be less trustworthy than predicted. It could also have been that in the initial plan his assignment was too simple: Thanks to his good relationship with the guards at the house-fortress, he had only to make them open the door, thus allowing the assailants led by Siqueiros to rush in. That night was Sheldon's turn to stand guard, and his disappearance was the only guarantee of a second chance. Killing Trotsky in his room would confirm that someone he knew had knocked on the door, while his kidnapping would foster the notion that he had probably been betrayed. The reaction of the defenders was quicker than the assailants had expected, which is why Siqueiros withdrew, uncertain of having achieved his objective. Mercader's noninvolvement would allow for a second attempt a few months later.

In March 1941 Vidali was arrested by men from the Mexican Security Service in the Alameda Central Park, while demonstrators from a right-wing group looked on from a distance. A foreigner also took part in the interrogation, and when he exchanged a few words in a low voice with the Mexican official, he revealed a marked North American accent.

"So what am I accused of?" Vidali asked.

The man who had been questioning him until then, a well-mannered young man in civilian clothes, smiled, glancing over at the fellow in the corner who was leaning against the wall, feigning complete disinterest.

"You are a guest in my country. And as you surely know, the law prohibits you from interfering in matters of internal politics."

"And walking through the Alameda would be a 'matter of internal politics'?" Vidali refuted, emphasizing the final words sarcastically.

The official picked up a slip of paper and showed it to him.

"This was in one of your pockets, right?"

"Yes, so?"

The man shook his head with the good-natured demeanor of someone scolding a small child.

"I could be mistaken, of course, but it looks to me like an index of names. There is a list with names of militants and sinarchist leaders, and we would like to know why you have written them down."

Vidali moved nervously, held back the curse that he was about to let out, and, fuming, said, "Come on, that's enough. I'm a journalist, and the least you could find in my pocket is a list of names. I came across that demonstration by accident, and I thought about writing an article. If you decide to ask serious questions, I would love to clarify any points. If not, I demand that Minister Téllez be informed at once. He can vouch for me and the work I am doing in this country."

On hearing the name of the minister of the interior, the stranger flinched almost imperceptibly. The Mexican official, on the other hand, winked, satisfied.

"This work of yours," the fellow with the American accent intervened, "also includes murdering political refugees whom your Party regards as adversaries or, if you prefer, 'traitors'?"

Vidali stared at him for a few seconds. Then he looked at the Mexican and asked, "May I ask who this man is and why I should answer his questions?"

"I just want to exchange a couple of words with you confidentially," the American quickly made clear. "You can very well refuse, as I have no authority to interrogate you. And, in a certain sense, I am not authorized to be here right now either."

Surprised, Vidali looked at the official and made a motion with his arms as if to ask what was going on. The young Mexican shrugged and said, "The gentleman works for the government of a friendly country, and what is more, considering the war taking place in Europe, it might not be long before we have to say an 'ally.' He asked me to do him the favor of putting him in touch with you and—we felt obliged to do so."

"And to exchange 'a couple of words' with an agent of U.S. counterespionage, was it necessary to detain me?" Vidali exclaimed.

"Let's say that it is preferable to avoid an official citation," the American intervened, grabbing a chair and sitting down across from him.

The two looked at each other for a long while, until the American took out a pack of cigarettes and offered him one. Vidali accepted, let him light it, and then exhaled the smoke in his face with his habitual defiant little smile. And he said out loud so that the Mexican could hear, "The national sovereignty of this country is in a most favorable situation."

"Please don't try to argue at any cost," the American said quietly. But he got up immediately, circled Vidali, and added, changing his attitude, "You work for the Soviet Union and can count on the complete support of the embassy. We don't want to interfere in Moscow's internal problems, and we demand the same of you."

Vidali reacted to the American's words with theatrical gestures of approval.

"We are also aware of your relationships with some representatives of the Mexican government, people whom we hold in high esteem, both personally and politically."

"Really?" Vidali said. "If it were up to people like you, the border with the United States would already be at Tierra del Fuego."

The fellow pretended not to hear him, and continued, "With everything we have found out up to now, we think that Leon Trotsky's murder was planned and organized in the United States, which should be considered a serious violation of the principle of nonintervention. We are not interested in your vendettas. And if I had to give my personal opinion, the more you slaughter one another, the less you will bother us."

Vidali got up abruptly, and the American stretched out his arms as if preparing to attack. But the official got up and banged on the desk. Then he motioned sharply for them to sit down.

"We know that you entered the United States again with false papers," the American went on. "And you did so repeatedly, violating the deportation order issued against you."

"Can you prove it?" Vidali interrupted.

"Don't worry about that. As soon as we have the necessary documentation, we will order your deportation."

Vidali exchanged looks with the official, who made a vague gesture to calm him down.

"I am here to offer you a way out," the American said, leaning forward. "Help us reconstruct the plan that was followed to carry out the murder—obviously the part that concerns my country—and we will forget about you and the part you played in the matter."

Vidali let out a derisive burst of laughter.

"Don't underestimate your 'friends,'" the other man continued in the same monotonous tone, "because if we were to decide to raise your case to the official level, you would find out, at your expense, what certain relationships are worth at a time when you might pose an embarrassing problem."

"If I am arrested," Vidali exclaimed, addressing the official, "I will explain my actions only before Mexican authorities."

"You don't realize that it is in your interest to avoid—"

"And you still don't understand that in order to question me a second time you must get a deportation order," Vidali said, standing up.

The American agent was still for a few seconds; then he looked at the official, who wore a resigned expression. He seemed not to know if he should say something or not; then he picked up the bag that he had left on the floor, put on his hat, and left, slamming the door.

The Mexican official motioned to Vidali as if asking what he was waiting for. When he was sure that the other man had gone, he approached him and said quietly, "Now then, don't you remember me?"

Vidali looked at him, surprised.

The young man stuck out his hand.

"I am the son of Senator Luis Monzón."

Vidali opened his mouth to say something, but shut up quickly when the man motioned.

"I head this section of the Security Service. I am sorry for everything that is happening, but it has been impossible for us to resist the pressure."

"What do you advise me to do?" Vidali asked, assuming a demeanor of compliance.

"Be patient, that's all. My government has already been informed; you needn't worry. The Soviet Embassy has received informal guarantees; everything is under control. But you have to give us time to reach a solution with the Americans. They don't care at all about—in short, about the events in Coyoacán. But they want to be absolutely certain that you won't bother them again in New York or in any other part of the United States. Do you understand?"

"I think so."

"Good. I'll have to hold you for a few days, long enough to make them happy, and in the meantime I'll think of something to satisfy them without harming you."

The incarceration of "Enea Sormenti" would not last long. Senator Luis Monzón was an old acquaintance of his, and his son, an officer in Mexican counterespionage, proved very skillful in deflecting the urgent requests from the agents in Washington. Moreover, Siqueiros, from his residence, mobilized all the influential political connections he could count on: In just a few hours he convened in his studio the president of the Republic himself, Ávila Camacho, who had recently succeeded Lázaro Cárdenas, and from whom he secured concrete guarantees regarding Vidali's fate.

Modotti remained closed up in her refuge and did not open her mouth when a Party militant went to see her to update her on the situation. Isabel Carbajal, the young Communist militant with whom Vidali had been living for several months, was in charge of maintaining Vidali's connections with the outside world. She managed to find a house near the prison in El Pocito, just a few meters from his cell window, and each day she brought him the latest news and carried back his messages for the Party leaders.

President Manuel Ávila Camacho ordered Vidali's release, and a few weeks later, he also found a solution for Siqueiros. Freeing him when not even one year had passed since the attack was impossible, but he obtained a special visa from the Chilean consul, Pablo Neruda, through which the sentence was commuted to temporary exile.

The minister of the interior, Ignacio García Téllez, took charge of putting the solution for the "Vidali case" into practice: He received him in his office and offered him new documents to normalize his situation in the country once and for all. In exchange he asked that the passports Vidali had used, which had enabled him to pass for an Uruguayan, an Austrian, a Peruvian, a Soviet, and a Spaniard, be destroyed. So, for the first time, his identity was confirmed as "Vidali, Vittorio, Italian, born in Muggia, journalist by profession."

Vidali could not refuse, but he understood that that "favor" was actually a discreet way of neutralizing him. Official recognition of his true identity meant limiting his work, forcing him not to hide behind the names of his countless passports. Freedom of movement became a subtle sentence for him: From that point on the whole world would know what his name and real business were, at least as long as he remained in Mexico.

The former Spanish minister Jesús Hernández had also chosen Mexico for his exile. One day he bumped into Modotti and told her of his definitive estrangement from the ideals that had led him to become a minister in the Spanish Republic. "Stalin and his band of assassins had transformed the word 'communist' into an insult." Then he told her that he had written his memoirs, which would soon be published, in which he denounced the different crimes of the GPU during the civil war. "I have also had to recount what Vidali did to Andrés Nin," he added, expecting some reaction from her. But she just nodded. However, when Hernández recalled that on a certain occasion he had had Vidali arrested after a violent confrontation with him, and that the GPU officials had ordered his immediate release, Modotti seemed unable to contain her anger and, with unexpected rancor she murmured, "You should have shot him. It would have been a good deed, I assure you. He is just a murderer—and he dragged me into a monstrous crime. I hate him with all my heart. And nevertheless, I am forced to follow him until the end. Until death."

Twenty-Eight

After many months of solitude, Modotti appeared again in public on New Year's Eve 1942, accepting Pablo Neruda's invitation to a dinner that was attended by close to a hundred people, including political figures from several countries and exiles from the Spanish civil war. Few recognized her, and she did what she could to go unnoticed.

A few days later, the evening of January 5, she went to dinner at the home of Hannes Meyer, who, having fled Nazi repression, had settled in Mexico City. The few close friends who gathered at the German architect's house considered it as a kind of farewell dinner for Modotti and Vidali, as everyone knew about Vidali's relationship with Carbajal. Vidali retired early, saying that he had some work to finish at *El Popular*.

Around midnight Modotti was not feeling well. She said that she wanted to go home and asked the painter Nacho Aguirre if he could get her a taxi. Aguirre was not an invited guest, but as he lived next door, Meyer had called him precisely because Modotti was there and he had not seen her since the days of Weston. At first Aguirre tried to persuade her to stay, thinking that it was just a passing indisposition. But she got up and headed for the door with such an agonized expression that he rushed to the street in order to stop the first taxi. He found one right out front, and when she was getting in he asked her if she wanted him to go with her. She shook her head no, forced a smile, and got into the car.

Meyer remembered Tina's last words as she left the house: "'Good-bye,' she said to me in Italian, after an evening in which we had spoken about the music of Shostakovich, about the war against the Nazis, about the possibility of a secret trip through Europe. Ten minutes later, she was lying in a taxi, motionless, cold and alone."

A police patrol found Tina Modotti's body inside a taxi that had been abandoned at the side of a road in the city center. The driver, who was located in the following days, would state that he had panicked when he discovered that the woman was dead.

According to a subsequent police version, the same taxi driver took her to the general hospital, since she had given him that address and not that of her home.

Modotti would later be identified by some friends. Vidali dropped out of circulation for a while: He was not among the few people who went to pay their respects at the funeral home, nor did he attend the funeral. He would justify his actions by saying that he had wanted to avoid a lynching by the press. In fact, the headline in the newspapers was matter-of-fact, TYPICAL STALINIST ELIMINATION, reporting that she could have been poisoned. During the first two days all the articles talked about "her former lover Carlos Contreras, whose real name seemed to be Enea Sormenti, merciless agent of the GPU, named as the one presumed responsible for Tina Modotti's murder." Her death was mentioned in connection with the unsolved murder of Julio Antonio Mella and with the more recent murder of Trotsky.

Influential journalists close to the Communist Party came out in Vidali's defense. Pablo Neruda himself, who in his role as Chilean consul was highly esteemed within Mexican governmental circles, released a poem entitled *Tina Modotti Has Died*, openly siding against the murder theory. After a blaze of accusations on all the front pages, Modotti's name suddenly disappeared from the newspapers the day after her funeral, which was attended by leaders of the Party and of syndicate organizations as well as representatives in an official capacity. The silence of the press could be explained by the delicate position Mexico found itself in, as it had sided against the Axis in the war that was taking place: The Soviet Union was an ally, and to point to its agents as assassins meant putting the government in a serious situation. Therefore the "Modotti case" did not exist: The medical report simply gave a heart attack as the cause of death, and no autopsy was performed because there was no evidence to suspect it had been murder.

A few years later her brother Benvenuto would speak out in an Italian-American newspaper to defend the idea that Tina had died of a heart attack: "My sister had come to spend two months in the United States and, before returning to Mexico, one night she said *addio* to me. 'Why *addio* and not *arrivederci?*' I asked her. She answered, 'Impossible. It is as if I were already dead. Down there in Mexico, I won't be able to survive.'" But that sentence, which Benvenuto took as proof that his sister knew she had a serious illness, could be interpreted in many ways.

One of the few people who had been in touch with her in the last few months did not discount the idea that it had been suicide. In a short time Modotti had become a shadow of the woman immortalized by Weston, the passive shell of all the pain caused by the most intense and violent period in this century. Worn out, exhausted, hopelessly sad and silent, destroyed by having lost the illusion of an ideal that power had transformed into paranoid madness, she might have chosen the only way to escape that slow daily death.

The cat disappeared among the rooftops, a Spanish friend of Modotti's took the dog, and Vidali married Isabel Carbajal, who would soon give birth to a son, Carlos. In the following years he would again be seen linked to dubious incidents and violent confrontations with representatives of the Stalinist opposition.

On January 11, 1943, in New York City, the syndicalist anarchist Carlo Tresca was killed by a gunshot; a few days earlier he had written a letter to his friend Marcel Pivert denouncing Vidali's presence and the defamatory campaign that he had unleashed against him in Communist circles. On April 1 numerous refugees of different nationalities gathered in the Mexican capital in order to commemorate Tresca's death. The meeting place, 50 Venustiano Carranza Street, was attacked by a group of armed Stalinists who destroyed the room and brutally attacked many of those present. The real objective seemed to have been Viktor Serge, whose name was shouted by some men who were carrying machine guns and pistols. The former POUM militant Juan Austrich managed to save Serge by dragging him into the kitchen, where he entrenched himself as shots riddled in the door. Vidali, to whom many pointed as one of the leaders of the commando squad, launched a smear campaign from the pages of *El Popular* affirming that from the windows of the meeting place came the cries of "Viva Franco! Viva Hitler!" and that the assailants were simply citizens angered by the outrage of those "enemies of the homeland."

As proof of premediation there were numerous telephone calls to the offices of all the newspapers minutes before the incident, placed by presumed "passersby" reporting a meeting of people of Nazi ideology on Venustiano Carranza Street.

Viktor Serge would die in 1947 of a heart attack, according to the forensic report. He was in a taxicab.

In the last few years an exhaustive study has been carried out to gather scientific data and direct testimony on the street laboratory set up by Yagoda, in which lethal substances capable of producing death "by natural causes" were prepared.

Moreover, those who defended political homicide in Viktor Serge's case maintained that in the 1940s the syndicate of taxi drivers was controlled by the Communist Party, which had used them to keep order at demonstrations and as bullies to carry out punitive missions.

Epilogue

Tina Modotti's tombstone is a rectangular gray stone damaged by time, lost in a corner of the vast Panteón de Dolores, on the northwestern edge of Mexico City. Anonymous friends bought it in 1942 and, because it was "perpetual," nobody has taken care of it since then. The grass surrounding it and growing out of its crevices is very tall. The dust and dead leaves make it hard to find. And to find out where it is, you have to look in the burial registry in the archives of the cemetery, one of the largest in the world. The bas-relief with Modotti's profile is barely visible, worn away by a half century of rain and wind. A crack runs across the top of the tombstone sunk in the ground, and the words of the last poem dedicated to her are barely legible, veiled by a film of moss:

> *Tina Modotti, sister, you do not sleep, no, you do not sleep.*
> *Perhaps your heart hears the rose of yesterday*
> *growing, the last rose of yesterday, the new rose.*
> *Rest gently, sister.*

The new rose is yours, the new earth is yours:
you have put on a new dress of deep seed
and your soft silence is filled with roots.
　　You shall not sleep in vain, sister.

Pure is your gentle name, pure is your fragile life.
Of bee, shadow, fire, snow, silence, foam,
of steel, line, pollen was built your tough,
　　your slender structure.

The jackal at the jewel of your sleeping body
still shows the white feather and the bloody soul
as if you, sister, could rise up,
　　smiling above the mud.

To my country I take you so that they will not touch you,
to my show country so that your purity
will be far from the assassin, the jackal, the Judas:
　　there you will be at peace.

Do you hear a step, a step-filled step, something
huge from the great plain, from the Don, from the cold?
Do you hear the firm step of a soldier upon the snow?
　　Sister, they are your steps.

They will pass one day by your little tomb
before yesterday's roses are withered,
the steps of tomorrow will pass by to see
　　where your silence is burning.

A world marches to the place where you were going, sister.
The songs of your mouth advance each day
in the mouths of the glorious people that you loved.
　　Your heart was brave.

In the old kitchens of your country, on the dusty
roads, something is said and passes on,
something returns to the flame of your golden people,
　　something awakes and sings.

Tina Modotti

They are your people, sister, those who today speak your name,
we who from everywhere, from the water and the land,
with your name leave unspoken and speak other names.
    Because fire does not die.

PABLO NERUDA
—From *Residence on Earth*

Selected Bibliography

Alexander, Robert J. *Trotskyism in Latin America.* Palo Alto, Calif.: Stanford University, Hoover Institute Press, 1973.

Anguino, A., G. Pacheco, and R. Vizcaíno. *Cárdenas y la izquierda mexicana* (Cárdenas and the Mexican left). Mexico City: Juan Pablos, 1984.

Brenner, Anita. *Idols Behind Altars.* Boston: Payson & Clarke, 1929.

Cahiers Leon Trotskij (Paris) 3 (July–Sept. 1979); 26 (June 1986).

Claraval, Bernardo. *Cuando fuí comunista.* Mexico City: Polis, 1944.

Conquest, Robert. *Il grande terrore* (The great terror). Milan, Italy: Mondadori, 1970.

Corneli, Dante. *Il redivivo tiburtino* (Man of Tivoli revived). Italy: La Pietra, 1977.

D'Attilo, Bob. "Glittering Traces of Tina Modotti." *Views* (Boston), 1985.

Deutscher, Isaac. *Stalin: Biografia politica* (Stalin: A political biography). Mexico City: Era, 1967.

Encuentro de la Juventud (Mexico City) 24 (Jan. 1986).

Gálvez Cancino, Alejandro. "Julio Antonio Mella: Un Marxista Revolucionario" (Julio Antonio Mella: A revolutionary Marxist). *Critica de la Economia Politica* 30, 1986.

Gordon, S., and T. Allan. *Il Bisturi e la Spada: Storia di Norman Bethune* (The scalpel and the shovel: The story of Norman Bethune). Milan, Italy: Feltrinelli, 1969.

Gorkin, Julián. *Canibales politicos* (Political cannibals). Mexico City, 1941.

———. *El proceso de Moscú en Barcelona* (The Moscow trial in Barcelona). Mexico City: Aymá, 1973.

Guerín, Daniel. *Ni dieu ni maître* (Neither god nor master). Paris, France: Maspero, 1970.

"La guerra di Spagna." *Storia Illustrata* 220, special issue; Mar. 1976.

Hernández, Jesús. *Yo fuí ministro de Stalin* (I was Stalin's ambassador). Mexico City, 1953.

Instituo Nacional de Bellas Artes.: Catalog of the Exhibition "Frida Kahlo." Texts by Testi de Raquel Tibol, Elena Poniatowska, Marti Casanova, Laura Mulvey, Peter Wollen, Carlton Beals.

Jackson, G. *La republica spagnola e la guerra civile* (The Spanish republic and the civil war). Milan, Italy: Il Saggiatore, 1979.

Jamis, Rauda. *Frida Kahlo.* Barcelona, Spain: Circe, 1988.

Karol, K. S. *Los guerrilleros en el poder* (Guerrillas in power). Madrid, Spain: Crítica, 1972.

Krivitski, W. G. *Sono stato agente di Stalin.* Milan, Italy: Mondadori, 1940.

Márquez, Fuentes M., and O. Rodríquez. *El partido comunista mexicano: 1919–1945* (The Mexican communist party: 1919–1945). Mexico City: El Caballito, 1973.

Martínez, Verdugo, A. *Historia del comunismo en Mexico* (The history of communism in Mexico). Mexico City, 1985.

Masutti, Nella. *Una piccola pietra* (One small stone). Rome, Italy: Editori Riuniti, 1982.

Medvedev, Roy A. *Lo Stalinismo: Origini, storia, conseguenze* (Stalinism: Origins, history, consequences). Milan, Italy: Mondadori, 1977.

Mella, Julio Antonio. *Escritos revolucionarios* (Revolutionary writings). Mexico City: Siglo XXI, 1978.

Mieli, Renato. *Togliatti 1937.* Milan, Italy: Rizzoli, 1964.

Nenni, Pietro. *Spagna.* Carnago (Varese), Italy: Sugarco, 1976.

Neruda, Pablo. "(Tina Modotti is dead.)" In *Residence en la tierra.* Buenos Aires, Argentina: Losada, 1973.

Newhall, Beaumont, and Nancy Newhall. *The Daybooks of Edward Weston.* New York: Aperture, 1961.

Nexos (Mexico City) 94 (Oct. 1985); 98 (Feb. 1986).

Nin, Andrés. *Guerra e rivoluzione in Spagna, 1931–1937* (War and revolution in Spain). Milan, Italy: Feltrinelli, 1974.

Nueva Antropología. (Havana, Cuba) 27 (July 1985).

Orwell, George. *Omaggio alla Catalogna* (Homage to Catalonia). Milan, Italy: Mondadori, 1982.

Pensamiento Crítico (Havana, Cuba) 39 (April 1970).

Proceso (Mexico City) 335, 344 (1983).

Richey, Roubaix de l'Abrie, and Tina Modotti. *The Book of Robo.* Los Angeles, Calif., 1923.

Robotti, Paolo. *La prova* (The exam). Dedalo, Italy: Bari, 1965.

Sánchez, Salazar, L. *Así asesinaron a Trotski* (Thus we assassinated Trotsky). Mexico City: Populibros la Prensa, 1955.

Seniga, Giulio. *Togliatti e Stalin.* Carngago (Varese), Italy: Sugarco, 1978.

Serge, Victor. *Carnets* (Notebooks). Arles, France: Actes Sud, 1985.

———. *Memorie di un rivoluzionario* (Memoirs of a revolutionary). Milan, Italy: Mondadori, 1983.

———. *Vita e morte di Trotzkij* (The life and death of Trotsky). Bari, Italy: Laterza, 1976.

Siempre (Mexico City) 894 (April 1979).

Spriano, Paolo. *I comunisti europei e Stalin* (The European communists and Stalin). Turin, Italy: Einaudi, 1983.

———. *I fronti populari, Stalin, la guerra* (The popular fronts, Stalin, the war). Vol. 3 of *Storia del partito communista italiano* (History of the Italian communist party). Turin, Italy: Einaudi, 1970.

Stasova, Elena. *Compagno absoljut* (The absolved companion). Rome, Italy: Riuniti, 1973.

Thomas, Hugh. *Storia della guerra civile spagnola* (The history of the Spanish civil war). Turin, Italy: Einaudi, 1975.

Tommasini, Umberto. *L'anarchico triestino* (Anarchy in Trieste). Italy: Antistato, 1984.

Torres, Edelberto. *Sandino.* Managua, Nicaragua: Editorial Nueva Nicaragua, 1983.

Trotsky, Leon. *Correspondance: 1933–1938.* Paris, France: Gallimard, 1980.

Tuñon de Lara, M. *Storia della repubblica e la guerra civile in Spagna* (The history of the republic and the civil war in Spain). Rome, Italy: Riuniti, 1966.

Universidad Veracruzana. *Tina Modotti* (exhibition catalog). Veracruz, Mexico: 1983.

Los Universitarios (Mexico City) 153–54, (Oct. 1979).

Vanni, Ettore. *Io comunista in Russia* (I was a communist in Russia). Bologna, Italy: Cappelli, 1949.

Venza, Claudio. *"La falsita continuano"* (The lies go on). *Volontà* 33, No. 6 (Nov. 1978).

Vidali, Vittorio. *Comandante Carlos.* Rome, Italy: Riuniti, 1983.

———. *Dal Messico a Murmansk* (From Mexico to Murmansk). Italy: Vangelista, 1976.

———. *Diario del xx congresso* (Diary of the twentieth congress). Italy: Vangelista, 1974.

———. *Giornale di borod* (Ship's log). Italy: Vangelista, 1977.

———. *Il 5 reggimento* (The fifth regiment). Italy: Vangelista, 1973.

———. *La caduta della repubblica* (The fall of the republic). Italy: Vangelista: 1979.

———. *Missione a Berlino* (Mission to Berlin). Italy: Vangelista, 1978.

———. *Ritratto di donna* (Portrait of a woman). Italy: Vangelista, 1982.

———. *Spagna lunga battaglia* (Spain's long struggle). Italy: Vangelista, 1975.

Wolfe, Bertram. *The Fabulous Life of Diego Rivera.* New York: Stein & Day, 1963.

Zaccaria, Guelfo. *A Mosca senza ritorno* (One way to Moscow). Carnago (Varese), Italy: Sugarco, 1983.

Index

Agelov, Silvia, 189, 190, 191
Agfa Paper, 46
Aguirre, Nacho, 202–203
anarchist movement
    Buenaventura Durruti and, 150–151
    Dino Modotti and, 61–62
    José Clemente Orozco and, 62
    Munich rebellion (1918) and, 30
    Nicola Sacco and Bartolomeo Vanzetti and, 54, 57
    in Spain, 142, 145, 150–152, 154, 155–157, 158, 173–174
Anti-Fascist League, in Mexico, 59, 61
Anti-Imperialist League of the Americas, 6
Arec, Mánuel Maples, 34

Aristocrats, The (Afinogenov), 140
"Army of Madmen," 92, 93
art, in Mexico
    as collective expression, 26, 29–30
    and photography, as political passion, 36, 88–90
    Soviet influence on, 49–50
    See also murals
Arzubide, Germán List, 32, 34, 94
At the End of the World (Zamyatin), 139
Austrich, Juan, 205
Averbach, Leopold, 137–138
Ayuda (newspaper), 171

Babich, Tony, 191
Baliño, Carlos, 65

Barcelona, Spain
anarchists vs. Marxists in,
155–157
at end of civil war, 173–174
Olympics in, 149
Barón, Ana María, 167–168
Bauhaus architecture, and
photography, 108
Bayer, Herbert, 108
Beimler, Hans, 153
Bell, Tom, 178
Berneri, Camillo, 158
Berzin, Jan Karlovic, 124, 170
Bethune, Norman, 148, 170–171
Bloodthirsty Russia (Vesely), 139
Blum, Léon, 177
Bordiga, Amadeo, 136
Bos, Evgenya Bogdanovna, 138
Bravo, Manuel Álvarez, 30, 32, 101
Brenner, Anita, 30, 36
British Journal of Photography, 46
Bronstein, Lev Davidovich. *See*
Trotsky, Leon
Browder, Earl, 181, 189, 192
Bukharin, Nikolay, 68, 69

Cabada, Juan de la, 30, 163
Calles, Plutarco Elías, 65, 69, 70
Calligaris, Luigi, 136–137
Camacho, Ávila, 200
Camara, Alfredo Pino, 3–6
Capa, Robert, 46, 164, 169
Carbajal, Isabel, 186, 200, 202,
204
Cárdenas, Lázaro, 182, 200
Carranza, Venustiano, 29, 49, 70
Carrillo, Rafael, 69, 71
Casamadrid, Alfonso, 3
Castaños, Virginia, 12

censorship, in Soviet Union,
139–140
Central Committee, of Communist
Party, 119–120
Chamberlain, Neville, 171
Chapingo, Universidad de, murals
of, 8, 29, 61
Charlot, Jean, 30, 31
Chauve-Souris, Le, 36–37
CISKA, of Communist Party Cen-
tral Committee, 119, 120
Codovilla, Victorio, 68, 69, 70,
161
Comintern (Communist International) and Hitler–Mussolini
collaboration, 158
influence of, in Mexico and Latin
America, 50, 68, 69
and intervention in Spain, 142,
146, 147, 149, 156, 159
and Nicaragua, 91, 95
Tina Modotti and, 148, 169–170
Vittorio Vidali and, 77
Commune of Paris and Dombrovsky,
149
Communism, and social revolution,
concepts of, 68, 69, 119,
146
Communist Party
Central Committee of, and
CISKA, 119–120
in Cuba, 65, 102
Diego Rivera and, 49–50, 71,
85–86, 87
in Germany, 106, 108, 112
in Italy, 136
in Latin America, 68, 69
in Mexico, 49, 53–54, 94–95, 98,
193, 205

in Spain, 145
in United States, 181
See also Comintern
(Communist International)
Confederación General de Traba-
jadores
(CGT), 70, 71
Confederación Nacional del Trabajo
(CNT), 145, 155, 156, 157
Confederación Regional Obrera
Mexicana (CROM), 65, 70,
71
Confederación Sindical Unitaria
Mexicana, 65, 71
Congreso de la Sindical Interna-
tional, 68
Contreras, Carlos. *See* Vidali,
Vittorio
Cooper, Jake, 183
Cornell, Charles, 183, 192
Creative Art, 46
Cuba
Communist Party in, 65, 102
Julio Antonio Mella and, 63,
64–65, 69, 71
Cueto, Germán, 33
cultural expression
and censorship, in Soviet Union,
139–140
and revolution, 29–30, 45–46,
164
Czechoslovakia, and Munich Pact,
171

Dalty, León, 153
Deladier (douard), 171
Denikin, Anton, 64
Deuxième Bureau, in France,
125–130, 171

Diario de viaje (Mella), 64
Díaz, Porfirio, 33
Dimitriev, Viktor, 138
Dimitrov Battalion, 150
documentary, social, and Tina
Modotti, 46
Dollfuss, Engelbert, 124
Dos Passos, John Roderigo, 164
Dromundo, Baltazar, 110–111
Duncan, Isadora, 138
Durruti, Buenaventura, 150–152
Durruti column, 150–151, 156
Dzhugashvili, Josif Vissarionovich.
See Stalin, Joseph

Eastman, Max, 139
Ehrenburg, Ilya, 151
Eisenstein, Sergei, 137
Ejercito del Sur, 49
Eleventh Division, in Spain, 163
Estridentism, 32–34
Excelsior (newspaper), 6–7, 8

Federacíon Anarquista Ibérica
(FAI), 145, 155, 156, 157
Fedin, Konstantin Aleksandrovich,
139
Fifth Regiment, in Spain, 147–149
Flores, Daniel, 101
Flores, José, 5
Forma (magazine), 36
Forty-sixth Division, in Spain,
157
France
Deuxième Bureau in, 125–130,
171
Red Aid activities in , 141, 178
and Spanish refugees, 177–178
Futurism, and Estridentism, 32

Gamboa, Fernando, 172–173
Ganivet, Paco, 174
García, Anastasio Somoza, 98
Garibaldi Antifascist Association, 193
Garro, Elena, 166–168
General Workers Union (UGT), 155
Germanetto, Giovanni, 122
Germany
    cultural and political life of (1930), 106–112
    and Nazi alliance with Stalinists, 146, 187
    Olympics in, 149
Gorkin, Julián, 152
Gorky, Maxim, 137, 139
GPU (Soviet secret police)
    Andrés Nin and, 159–161
    and Kirov assassination, 135, 136
    and Soviet censorship, 140
    in Spanish civil war, 152, 153, 154, 158, 201
    Trotsky assassination and, 183, 189, 195–196
    Vittorio Vidali and, 129, 203
Grisha. See Berzin, Jan Karlovic
Guarnaschelli, Emilio, 122
Guerra di classe (newspaper), 158
Guerrero, Elisa, 42, 66
Guerrero, Xavier
    as artist, 39, 49, 50–51
    Communist Party allegiance of, 49, 50, 51, 71
    Diego Rivera and, 29, 50–51
    in Moscow, 62, 66–67, 116–117
    and revolutionary militancy, 39–40

Tina Modotti and, 7, 29, 39–40, 44, 51–52, 62, 66–67, 116–117

Hafkina, Paulina, 116
Hagemeyer, Johan, 27–28
Hands Off Nicaragua Committee, 67, 91, 94
Harte, Robert Sheldon, 183, 184, 196
Hatfield, G. D., 93
Heartfield, John, 108
Hemingway, Ernest, 163, 164
Herberiche, Luis, 2, 6
Hernán, Gustavo Ortiz, 89–90
Hernández, Jesús, 159–161, 201
Hitler, Adolph
    and Joseph Stalin, 153, 187
    and Munich Pact, 171
Homage to Catalonia (Orwell), 157
Horizonte (magazine), 34
Huerta, Victoriano, 29, 33
Huston, John, 31
Huxley, Aldous, 139

Ibarruri, Dolores, 172
Incógnito, Lo (Weston), 34
Indio de Niquinohomo, 92–93
Industrial Workers of the World (IWW), 18
International Brigades, in Spain
    Buenaventura Durruti, 150–151
    dissolution of, 171
    and the Gestapo, 160–161
    and Soviet intervention, 146, 154, 161
International Congress for the Defense of Culture against Fascism, Second, 163

International Congress of the Syndical Organization, 65

International Red Aid. *See* Red Aid, International

Irradiador (magazine), 34

Italian Communist Party, 136

Italian Emigrants, Club of, in Moscow, 121–123, 136–137

Italian government
  and Italians, in Moscow, 121–123, 136–137, 178
  Tina Modotti and, 61–62, 104–105, 111
  troops of, in Spain, 170
  See also OVRA (Italian Secret Police)

Ivanov, Vsevolod Vyacheslvovich, 139

Jackson, Frank. *See* Mercader del Rio, Ramon

Jacobi, Lotte, 110, 137

Junco Sandalio, 69, 76

Justice and Liberty Movement, 149

Juventud (magazine), 65

Kahlo, Frida
  Diego Rivera and, 83–87
  early life of, 81–82
  Leon Trotsky and, 182–183

Kerley, Walter, 183

Kirov (Sergei Mironovich Kostricov), 134, 135–136

Kisch, Egon Erwin, 110

Kollontai, Alexandra, 169–170

Kornaciuk, Hava, 143

Kornaciuk, Ivan, 143–144

Koska, Willy, 131

Kostricov, Sergei Mironovich (Kirov), 134, 135–136

Krivitsky, W. G., 153–154

Lafayette shooting squadron, 150

Landa, Matilde, 174

La Tierra (Rivera), 8

League of Nations, and International Brigades, 171

Lecoeur, Auguste, 151–152

Ledesma, Gabriel Fernández, 36

Lenin (Vladimir Ilich Ulyanov), 64, 68

Leyda, Jay, 137

Lincoln Brigade, in Spanish civil war, 149

Lister, Enrique, 159, 163, 172, 190

Literature and Revolution (Serge), 137

Llano, Rodrigo de, 8

Longo, Luigi, 120, 121

Lopez, Rafael, 33

Lorenzo, Rosendo Gómez, 62, 63

Lunacharsky, Anatoly Vasilyevich, 50

Machado, Antonio, 178

Machado, Gerardo, 4, 7, 65, 76, 86

Machado, Gustavo, 94

Machete, El (newspaper)
  David Alfaro Siqueiros and, 29–30
  Moscow direction of, 51, 98–99
  Tina Modotti and, 45, 51, 61, 62

Mackenzie-Papinau Regiment, in Spanish civil war, 149

Magriñat, Jose, 9–11, 12

Malraux, André, 150, 163, 164

Man, Tom, 149

Marín, Federico, 30, 31

Marín, Lupe, 30, 31, 86

Martí, Agustín Farabundo, 94, 98, 99

Martínez, Ricardo, 69, 70

Matthias, Leo M., 42, 112

Mayakovski, Vladimir, 39, 115, 138

Mella, Julio Antonio
 and Andrés Nin, 68, 69
 character and personality of, 66, 67
 death of, 1–13, 75–76, 203
 Diario de viaje of, 64
 Diego Rivera and, 8, 71
 and Leon Trotsky, 67, 68–69, 70, 90
 and Nicaragua, 94
 political activism of, and Communist Party, 63, 64–71
 Tina Modotti and, 1–13, 62–63, 66, 67, 72–76, 90

Menotti, Clarenzo, 122

Mercader del Río, Caridad, 195

Mercader del Río, Ramón, 189–192, 195–196

Mexican Communist Party (Partida Comunista Mexicana - PCM)
 and Cuban relations, 69
 founding of, 49
 Leon Trotsky and, 193
 and Nicaragua, 94–95, 98
 and social revolution, concepts of, 68–69
 Soviet Union, relationship with, 69
 Vittorio Vidali and, 53–54, 205

Mexican Folkways, 62, 90

Mexican revolution, and Estridentism, 33

Mexico
 colonialism in, 38–39
 revolutionary atmosphere of, 23, 26, 29–30
 and Soviet Union, contrast of, 50
 Tina Modotti's relationship with, 36, 37, 38

Meyer, Hannes, 108, 202, 203

Mije, Antonios, 150

Modotti, Benevenuto, 20, 61, 204

Modotti, Dino, 61–62

Modotti, Giuseppe (brother), 20

Modotti, Giuseppe (father), 17, 18, 26

Modotti, Mercedes, 18, 162–163

Modotti, Tina (Assunta Adelaide Luigia Modotti)
 as actress, 18, 20, 36–37
 in Berlin, 106–112
 as Carmen Ruiz Sánchez, 174, 179, 180
 death of, 202–205, 206
 deportation of, and arrival in Europe, 101–105
 descriptions of, 13, 17–18, 20, 31, 34, 37, 41, 42, 52, 159, 173, 194
 Diego Rivera and, 8–9, 29, 39, 43, 83–84, 86–87, 170
 Edward Weston and, 8, 21–23, 28–31, 34, 35–38, 41–45, 59–60, 118, 170, 180
 Elena Garro and, 166–168
 Estridentism and, 32–34
 family of, and early life, 17–19, 20–21, 27, 42, 61–62, 162–163

Frida Kahlo and, 81–87
and Italian government, 60–62,
  104–105, 111, 162, 178
Julio Antonio Mella and, 1–13,
  62–63, 66, 67, 72–76, 90, 117
letters of, to Edward Weston, 38,
  39, 42–43, 44–45, 60, 76–77,
  102–104, 107–108, 109–110,
  117–118
as María, 148, 154, 172, 181
in Mexico (1923–1930), 25–26,
  29–46, 51–52, 53–58, 66–67,
  69–73, 72–77, 83–85, 86–87,
  88–90, 91, 95–97, 101
in Moscow, 115–118, 120–121,
  124–125, 136, 137, 141–144
and Nicaragua, 91, 95–97
and nostalgia for Italy, 53, 178,
  193
in Paris, 125, 130–133, 141,
  178
as photographer, 21, 27, 28, 32,
  34, 35, 36, 39, 42–43, 45–46,
  51, 60, 67, 72–73, 88–90, 104,
  107–110, 137, 188, 194
photographic exhibitions of, 36,
  41, 43, 88–90, 110
as Red Aid worker in Europe,
  124, 125, 126, 141, 153, 171,
  172
and return to Mexico (1939),
  179–181, 185–188, 193–194,
  202–205, 206
as Rose Smith Santarini, 3
Roubaix de l'Abrie Richey (Robo)
  and, 19, 21, 22, 23–24, 25–26
social revolution, and art, atti-
  tudes toward, 36, 38, 39, 51,
  88–90, 104

in Spain, 148, 153, 159,
  162–168, 169–174
Vittorio Vidali and, 53–58, 77,
  95–97, 102, 104, 105, 112,
  115, 118, 120–121, 124–133,
  163–166, 170–172, 177–181,
  185–188, 200, 201, 202
  Xavier Guerrero and, 29, 39–40,
    44, 51–52, 62, 66–67,
    116–117
Modotti, Valentina, 20–21
Modotti, Yolanda, 17–18, 20
Moholy-Nagy, László, 108
Molotov, Vyackeslev, 146
Monroe Doctrine, 38, 92
Monzón, Luis, 199, 200
Mora, Constancia de la, 188, 194
Mornard, Jacques. See Mercader del
  Río, Ramon
Morrow, Dwight, 101
Movimento Estridentista, 32–34
Mundo Obrero, 161
Munich Pact, 171
murals
  at Chapingo, 8, 29, 51
  as collective expression, 30
  Estridentism and, 33
  José Clemente Orozco and, 62,
    137
  and revolutionary militancy, 39
  Siqueiros's manifesto on, 29
  in Soviet Union, 50
Mussolini, Benito, 171
Mussolini alla conquista delle
  Baleari (Berneri), 158

National Socialism, 106
National Solidarity Congress
  (Madrid), 171, 172

Nazism
  growth of, in Germany, 106, 109
  Soviet Union and, 146, 187
  Spanish civil war and, 178
Negrín, Juan López, 171
Neruda, Pablo
  as Chilean consul, in Mexico,
    201, 202, 203
  poem for Tina Modotti, 206–208
  in Spain, 163
New Emigrants in Cuba, National
  Association of, 69
Nicaragua
  Hands Off Nicaragua Committee,
    67, 91, 94
  U.S. occupation of, 91–95
Nikolayev, Leonid, 135
Nin, Andrés
  death of, 159–161, 167, 201
  and "Leftist Opposition," 68, 69
  No Pasarán (Paz), 106

Óbregon, Álvaro, 26, 70
Ocotal, Batttle of, 93
Orozco, José Clemente, 29, 62, 137
Orwell, George, 139, 156–158
OVRA (Italian secret police)
  and Dino Modotti, 61–62
  and Tina Modotti, 61, 104, 111,
    162
  and Vittorio Vidali, 53, 128

Panama Canal, 91–92
Pan-American Conference, Sixth,
  69
Pan-Pacific International Exhibition, 19
Panteón de Dolores (Mexico City),
  25, 206

Partida Comunista Mexicana (PCM)
  and Cuban relations, 69
  founding of, 49
  Leon Trotsky and, 193
  and Nicaragua, 94–95, 98
  social revolution, concepts of,
    68–69
  Soviet Union, relationship with,
    69
  Vittorio Vidali and, 53–54,
    205
Partido Obrero de Unidad Marxista
  (POUM), 146, 152, 153, 155,
    156, 157, 159
Partido Socialista Unificado de
  Cataluña (PSUC), 152, 153
Pasternak, Boris, 139
Paz, Octavio, 166, 167, 168,
    189–190
photography
  appeal of, in Mexico, 26
  in Germany, 107, 108
  and social revolution, 36, 88–90
  See also Modotti, Tina: as pho-
    tographer
Picelli, Guido, 152–153
Pilnyak, Boris (Boris Andreyevich
  Vogau), 139
Pivert, Marcel, 204
Plaza, Salvador de la, 94
Popular, El (newspaper), 181,
    205
Popular Front, in France, 177
Porfiristas, 33
Pound, Ezra, 45
Pravda (newspaper), 156, 163
Prensa, La (newspaper), 13
Proletarian Writers, Association of,
    137

Que viva México (Eisenstein), 137
Quintana, Valente, 12

Rakosi group, in Spain, 149
Ramíriz, Díaz, 69
Red Aid, International
    Ayuda and, 171
    in Eastern Europe, 124
    France, 125, 126, 162, 178
    in Mexico and Latin America, 59,
        180
    in Moscow, 117
    original purpose of, 59
    in Spain, 147, 153, 166, 171,
        172
    in Switzerland, 110
    transformation of, 153
Reed, Alma, 137
Residence on Earth (Neruda), 206–
    208
revolution
    cultural expression and, in Mex-
        ico, 29–30, 45–46
    social concepts of, 68, 69,146
Revolutionary Syndicate of Techni-
    cal Workers, Painters, and
    Sculptors, 29–30
Rexroth, Kenneth, 52
Ribbentrop, Joachim von, 146
Richey, Roubaix de l'Abrie (Robo)
    character of, 19
    and Edward Weston, 21, 24
    in Mexico, 23–24, 26
    and Tina Modotti, 21, 22, 24,
        25–26, 101
Rien, Mark, 153
Río, Caridad Mercader del, 195
Río, Ramon Mercader del, 189–192,
    195–196

Rivera, Diego
    Communist Party and, 49–50,
        71, 85–86, 87
    Estridentism and, 33
    Frida Kahlo and, 83–87
    Leon Trotsky and, 87, 182–183
    Mexican artistic movement and,
        29–30, 85
    murals of, 29, 33, 50–51
    Tina Modotti and, 8–9, 29, 39,
        43, 83–84, 86–87, 170
Robbins, Harold, 183
Robelo, Ricardo Gómez, 31
Robotti, Paolo, 122–123
Rodchenko, Alexander, 108
Rodríquez, Anacleto, 5
Rosselli, Carlo, 149
Rovira, José, 152
Rubio, Pascual Ortiz, 81, 100

Sacco, Nicola, 54, 57
Salvemini, Gaetano, 158–159
Sánchez, Carmen Ruiz. See Modotti,
    Tina
Sandinismo, 98
Sandinista guerrillas, 93, 94
Sandino, Augusto César, 67, 91–99
Santarini, Rose Smith. See Modotti,
    Tina
Schüssler, Otto, 183
Sedova, Natalia, 182–183, 192
Semana, La (newspaper), 9
Serge, Viktor, 137, 140, 205
Seymour, David, 46, 169
Sindical Unitaria Mexicana, Con-
    federación, 65, 71
Siqueiros, David Alfaro
    Mexican artistic movement and,
        29–30

Siqueiros, David Alfaro (*cont'd*)
  Mexican Communist Party and,
    49–50, 69
  in Spanish civil war, 163
  Tina Modotti and, 88
  and Trotsky assassination,
    183–185, 189–190, 193, 196,
    201
  Vittorio Vidali and, 200
Sobol, Andrei, 138
Socialism, National, in Germany,
  106
socialist revolution, opposing concepts of, 68, 69, 146
Somoza García, Anastasio, 98
Sorge, Richard, 124–125
Sormenti, Enea. *See* Vidali, Vittorio
Soviet Union
  and aid to fascist Italy, 158
  censorship in, 139–140
  and counterespionage, 153–154
  cultural environment of, 137–140
  and Mexico, relationship with,
    39, 204
  military secret police in, 124–125
  political climate of, for Italians,
    119–123, 136
  and purges (1934), 134–137,
    141–142, 144
  and Spanish civil war, 142,
    145–154, 155–157, 159,
    177–178
  See also Communist Party; Com-
    intern (Communist Interna-
    tional); GPU (Soviet Secret
    Police); Stalin, Joseph
Sozzi, Gastone, 61, 149
Spanish civil war, 145–154
  end of, 170–174, 177–178

  and Italian troops, 170
  and Soviet involvement, 142,
    145–154, 155–157, 159,
    177–178
Stachel, Jack, 189, 191, 192
Stalin, Joseph
  and Leon Trotsky, 49, 67–68,
    157, 179, 183
  and Nicaragua, 95, 98
  purges by (1934), 134–136,
    137–140, 144
  and revenge, taste for, 71
  Spanish civil war and, 145, 146,
    153–154, 156, 157
Stasova, Elena, 115–116, 125,
  178
Stirner (Edgar Woog), 69, 71
Syndical Organization, International Congress of, 65
Syndicate, Revolutionary, of Technical Workers, Painters, and
  Sculptors, 29–30

Taro, Gerda, 46, 169
Technical Workers, Painters, and
  Sculptors, Revolutionary Syn-
  dicate of, 29–30
Tejeda, Adalberto, 180
Téllez, Ignacio García, 197, 201
Thaelmann, Ernst, 149
Tierra, La (Rivera), 8
Tina Modotti Has Died (Neruda),
  203
Togliatti, Palmiro, 122, 147, 149,
  159, 161, 172
Tolón, Rogelio Teurbe, 11–12
Tolstoy, Aleksey, 139
Tommasini, Umberto, 158
Torsvan, Berick. *See* Traven, Bruno

Traven, Bruno, 30–31, 193–194
Treasure of the Sierra Madre, The (Traven), 31
Tren Blindado (magazine), 67
Tresca, Carlo, 204
Trotsky, Leon
  assassination of, 147, 154, 183–185, 189–193, 198, 203
  children of, 183, 184
  Diego Rivera and, 87, 182–183
  Joseph Stalin and, 49, 67–68, 157
  Julio Antonio Mella and, 67, 68–69, 70, 90
  in Mexico, 182–185
  as Red Army commander, 64
Trotskyism
  and "permanent revolution," 67–68, 146
  in Spain, 142, 146, 153, 156
  Stalin's aversion to, 157
Twenty-ninth Division, in Spain, 157

UGT, in Spain, 146
Ulyanov, Vladimir Ilich. *See* Lenin
Unionfoto GMBH, 109
United States
  and Modotti files, 181
  and Nicaraguan invasion, 67, 91–95, 98
  and Pancho Villa, 70
  and Trotsky assassination, 179, 196–200
Universal Gráfico, El, 89
Universal Ilustrado, El, 39
Universidad de Chapingo, and murals, 8, 29, 51

Universidad Nacional Autónoma de México, 89
Universidad Popular José Martí, 65
Us (Zamyatin), 139

Valentino, Rodolfo, 20
Vanzetti, Bartolomeo, 54, 57
Variétés, 46
Vasconcelos, José, 26, 30, 31, 81
Vasilyev, Pavel, 140
Vesely, Artem, 139
Vidali, Vittorio
  Andrés Nin and, 160–161, 201
  Buenaventura Durruti and, 151
  Camillo Berneri and, 158
  as Carlos Contreras, 102, 128, 171, 180, 193, 203
  Carlo Tresca and, 204
  character of, 147
  as Enea Sormenti, 53, 128, 200, 202, 203
  and escape to Europe, 102, 104, 105
  in France and U.S. (1939), 177–181
  Isabel Carbajal and, 186, 200, 202, 204
  as Jacobo Hurwitz Zender, 102
  in Mexico (1939–1941), 180–181, 185–188, 196–201
  in Moscow, 115, 117, 118, 119–123, 136, 141–144
  and Nicaragua, 95–97
  in Paris, 124–133, 178
  in Spain, 142, 146–149, 158, 159, 163–166, 169, 170, 171–174

Vidali, Vittorio (*cont'd*)
  Tina Modotti and, 53–58, 77,
    95–97, 102, 104, 105, 112,
    115, 118, 120–121, 124–133,
    163–166, 170–172, 177–181,
    185–188, 200, 201, 202, 203
  and Trotsky assassination, 193
Villa, Francisco (Pancho), 39, 70
Villistas, 70
Vittorio, Giuseppe de, 159, 178
Voce degli italiani, La (Vittorio),
  159
Vogau, Boris Andreyevich. *See*
  Pilnyak, Boris
Volkow, Vsevolod, 184
Voroshilov, Kliment, 125
Vyshinski, Andrey Yanuaryevich,
  165

Walker, William, 91
Weil, Ruby, 189
Weston, Brett, 41, 44
Weston, Chandler, 29, 38
Weston, Edward
  family and early life of, 22–23
  Lázló Moholy-Nagy and, 108
  letters to, 38, 39, 42–43, 44–45,
    60, 76–77, 102–104, 107–108,
    109–110, 117–118
  and Mexican culture, 29, 30
  as photographer, 21, 22, 60
  photographic exhibitions of, 26,
    28, 43
  and Tina Modotti, 8, 21–23,
    28–31, 34, 35–38, 41–45,
    59–60, 118, 170, 180
Weston, Flora May Chandler, 22–23
Williard, Marcel, 178
Woog, Edgar (Stirner), 69, 71
Wrangel, Pyott, 64

Yagoda, 138, 205
Yesenin, Sergei, 138

Zagorsky, Vladimir, 122
Zamyatin, Yevgeny Ivanovich,
  139
Zapata, Emiliano, 39, 49
Zapatistas, 70
Zender, Jacobo Hurwitz. *See* Vidali,
  Vittorio
Zwaart, Piet, 108

About the Author and Translator

Pino Cacucci lives in Bologna, Italy, and is the author of several works of fiction, two of which have become popular Italian films. He is also an established journalist, travel writer, and translator of Spanish. He received the Kodak Award for Biographies of Photographers in 1989 and the Nonfiction Award from the Noir In Festival in 1992 for the Italian edition of *Tina*.

Patricia J. Duncan received a B.A. in Spanish Language and Literature from Duke University and an M.A. in Hispanic Civilization from New York University in Madrid, Spain. She is the author of a book on learning English as a second language for the Spanish-speaking community, entitled *Ingles Hecho Facil*, as well as a biography of Sammy Sosa. In addition, she has translated the work of Mexican authors David Toscana and Martha Cerda, as well as the Argentine author Mempo Giardinelli. She is also author of a bilingual biography of the actress Salma Hayek, forthcoming from St. Martin's Press. She lives in San Francisco.